STUDIES IN ECONOMICS AND BUSINESS

Financial Management

Leslie Chadwick MBA FCCA Cert.Ed

University of Bradford School of Management

Series Editor
Susan Grant
West Oxfordshire College

Heinemann

Heinemann Educational Publishers
Halley Court, Jordan Hill, Oxford, OX2 8EJ
a division of Reed Educational and Professional Publishing Ltd

OXFORD MELBOURNE AUCKLAND
JOHANNESBURG BLANTYRE GABORONE
IBADAN PORTSMOUTH (NH) USA CHICAGO

Heinemann is a registered trademark of Reed Educational and Professional Publishing Ltd

Text © Leslie Chadwick, 2001

First published in 2001
05 04 03 02 01
10 9 8 7 6 5 4 3 2 1

British Library Cataloguing in Publication Data
A catalogue record for this book is available from the British Library

ISBN 0 435 33218 X

Typeset by J&L Composition Ltd, Filey, North Yorkshire
Printed and bound in Great Britain by Biddles Ltd, Guildford

Acknowledgements
The publishers would like to thank the following for permission to reproduce copyright
material: AQA examination questions are reproduced by permission of the Assessment and
Qualifications Alliance; Atlantic Syndication and *The Daily Mail*, p.3; OCR examination
questions reproduced with the kind permission of OCR.

The publishers have made every effort to contact copyright holders. However, if any material has been incorrectly acknowledged, the publishers would be pleased to correct this at the
earliest opportunity.

Tel: 01865 888058 www.heinemann.co.uk

Contents

Preface

This book has been specially designed and written to meet the needs of A Level and AS Level students studying financial management. In particular, it covers the accounting and finance requirements of:

- AQA Module 1 & A2 Module 4
- OCR AS Module 2872 and A2 Module 2875
- Edexcel Unit 3 and A2 Unit 4 and Unit 5.5.

Students who are studying for VCE, HND, Business Studies courses, and other University or College courses which require a knowledge of accounting and finance should find this text to be a very useful addition to their bookshelf.

The principal strengths of this book are that it is readable, user-friendly, concise, and provides a variety of self-learning material. It aims to develop both numeric (computational) and written (comprehensional) skills, and includes:

- mini real world case studies and press cuttings
- step by step examples
- worked examples
- essay topics.

Leslie Chadwick is regarded as one of the UK's leading authors in accounting and finance. His books are now published and sold around the world and some have been translated into other languages. He is a senior lecturer in accounting and finance and the head of work experience placements at the University of Bradford School of Management. He has lectured and made presentations in the UK and overseas to AS and A Level students, undergraduates, postgraduates, managers and executives.

Susan Grant
Series Editor

Introduction

Financial management is fundamental

A child's eye view of an accountant could be 'an accountant sits at the top of an ivory tower and counts out the money'. When asked for their perceptions about accountants other people of more mature years may reply, 'someone who is good at maths' or 'they fiddle the tax' or 'it is difficult to understand what they are talking about' or simply 'boring!' There is an element of truth in some of the remarks. Accountancy and financial management are about the management of money (cash flow), the language of accounting (terminology) is a minefield, and accountants do try to keep their clients' tax liability to a minimum within the law.

Both private and public sector organizations need financial management. All companies, banks, building societies, charities, sole traders, partnerships, government departments (local, regional or national), the European Union etc. rely on their accounting and finance functions to supply them with information which will help with decision making and in monitoring and controlling operations. It is a fundamental part of any organization, however small. It is concerned with the management of scarce resources, recording systems, auditing, the computation of profits or losses, the net worth in terms of assets and liabilities, reporting and assessing financial performance, financing decisions, investment decisions, dividend policy, take-overs, tax matters, bankruptcy and liquidations etc.

Our aim

We aim to assist you in achieving your goal by providing you with a concise user-friendly overview of the subject. The material has been designed to help you develop your numerical, written and critical evaluation/reflective learning skills and to make you aware of the problems/limitations which may be encountered.

Chapter One
An introduction to financial management

'Employers tend to be impressed if I know something about accounting.'
'I want to be able to look at a set of accounts and understand them.'
Leslie Chadwick, *Essential Financial Accounting for Managers*, Financial
Times Prentice Hall, 2001.

Introducing financial management
The term 'accountancy' can be sub-divided into a number of different
divisions, the major divisions are: **financial accounting, cost and management
accounting** and **financial management**. Although the title of this
text is *Financial Management*, it does cover the other two areas. Indeed, it
is extremely difficult to define where each of the divisions starts and finishes.
Figure 1 provides you with an overview of the accounting scene.

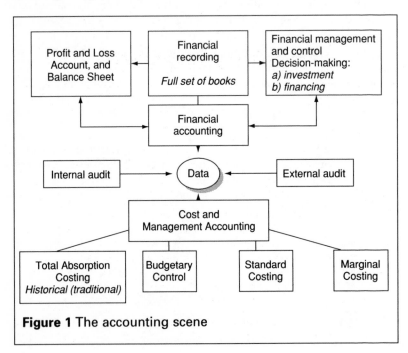

Figure 1 The accounting scene

Financial accounting

Financial accounting is concerned with the **financial recording system**, for example the ledger accounts kept on hard-drive and discs to store and accumulate the information needed to prepare the accounts such as the sales account. In addition, the financial accounting function may also be responsible for **credit control,** which aims at collecting the cash owing from credit customers (the debtors) as quickly as possible. Much of what is produced is **historic**, for example, the **statutory report and accounts** which are published after the year end.

Cost and management accounting

A vast amount of the information which is used has to be **pre-determined,** i.e. it is based on estimated figures, for example budgetary control. It aims to produce relevant information and advice for management which will help them with their decision-making, planning, monitoring, controlling of the business, setting corporate objectives and policy formulation.

The following press cutting highlights the problems of forecasting future costs and revenues for long-term contracts. Since publication of the article, the proposed plans have changed and changed again.

Wembley Stadium II

When plans were put forward in 1996 it was estimated that £240m would cover the cost of the new Wembley Stadium. A year ago the cost had rocketed to £475m. Now it is £660m and rising.

A financial source who saw the latest business plan presented by Wembley's owners to the banks in their quest to borrow £410m said, 'The figures are spiralling and the banks appear to be less and less interested in getting involved'. He added, 'The project was meant to capture the public's imagination, like the Millennium Dome was, but appears to be worryingly ambitious'. The £125m rise in costs was equivalent to the entire bill for Cardiff's Millennium Stadium and half the cost of the Sydney centrepiece which was used in the 2000 Olympics.

Interest charges on the loan needed to build the new Wembley will be between £40m and £60m a year, despite the old stadium making £15m a year.

Wembley National Stadium Ltd (WNSL) claim that the 90,000-seater stadium will generate more than £70m when it opens in 2004 and that corporate entertainment, a four-star hotel, office space and banqueting halls will boost the income.

Adapted from '£660 Wembley woe. Stadium plan in new trouble as cost soars' by Peter Allen, *Daily Mail*, 2 December 2000.

Financial management

Financial management nowadays has become a very wide area. Two of the principal areas which are of particular relevance to us are **financing decisions** which are concerned with the sources of business finance, and **investment decisions** which includes capital investment appraisal (project appraisal).

From a review of Figure 1 it can be observed that there is also the auditing function which can be carried out by internal (employees of the company/organization) and external auditors (firms of accountants). For example, public limited companies are required by law to include an **Auditors' Report** in their statutory published annual report and accounts (published accounts). The reports (Figure 2) have to certify whether or not the accounts give a true and fair view of the profit or loss for the year and a true and fair view of the state of affairs as shown in the Balance Sheet.

Report of the auditor to the members of Leswik plc

Opinion

In our opinion, the accounts give a true and fair view of the state of affairs of the company and the group as at 31 December 20X4 and of the profit of the group for the year then ended and have been properly prepared in accordance with the Companies Act 1985 and 1989.
GWXG Audit Plc
Chartered accountants
Registered auditor,
Money Row Plaza,
Beck Ham
5th March, 20X5

Figure 2 Specimen auditors' report

The users of accounting information and their needs

There are many parties (sometimes referred to as 'the stakeholders') interested in the accounts and financial performance of companies. Many of them are interested in **profitability**, i.e. their return on investment (ROI, which may also be described as ROCE, return on capital employed). Most are also very interested in **liquidity**, i.e. the ability to pay the debts owing by the company, for example, to creditors for goods and services which were supplied on credit. Cash flow problems could cause a company to go out of business. Certain groups or individuals could be monitoring the share prices, dividend payouts and ratios such as interest cover, the price/earnings ratio (PE ratio), gearing and efficiency ratios. We will review these and other ratios in Chapter 6. Figure 3 below will help you to appreciate the needs of some of the principal users.

USER	THEIR NEEDS
Management	Financial performance – in particular the productivity of the capital employed (ROI, ROCE), liquidity, efficiency measures such as debtor days (how long it takes them to collect their debts), interest cover and gearing. Other information such as project appraisals, cash budgets (cash flow forecasts), capital expenditure budgets, product costs, the cost of a service, and so on.
Shareholders	The ROI (return on investment). Liquidity. Share prices, dividend payout, price earnings ratio, gearing.
Loan creditors	Liquidity. Interest cover. The gearing. The valuation of fixed assets, for example, land and buildings and the amount which has been pledged as security for existing loans and debentures (a special type of loan).
Other creditors	Liquidity. Also the value of fixed assets pledged as security and the level of gearing. They want to be sure they will get paid.
Tax authorities	That the accounts do give a true and fair view. To ensure that the accounting policies have been applied on a fair and consistent basis, for example, the value of stocks and work in progress, the treatment of depreciation etc. For certain types of business the gross profit to sales ratio and other ratios.

Figure 3 The needs of the users of financial information

There are other users of financial information which include government departments (both local and national), bankers, competitors, customers and society at large. Various users could also be quite interested in the non-financial information contained in the published accounts and the financial press, for example, the Directors' Report, matters relating to social responsibility and 'green issues', movements of key personnel, details of new products and services, the outlook for the future, and so on.

Legal matters

Legislation relating to charities, solicitors, partnerships, banks, building societies, local government, and so on dictate and specify accounting requirements. For example, regulations relating to liquidity for banks, the way in which the accounts of clients should be kept by solicitors, the right of access to local government accounts.

In the UK the principal legislation which affects companies are **The Companies Acts 1985 and 1989.**

The business environment

The environment in which businesses and organizations operate is both complex and diverse. Changes in the environment can have a significant impact on the bottom line (i.e., the profit or loss figure). Changes in the basic assumptions about the future may render the plans, targets and budgets useless. For example, changes in the rate of inflation, levels of output, pay settlements, market expectations, and so on. Figure 4 provides you with a simple but comprehensive overview of the environment in which all businesses have to operate.

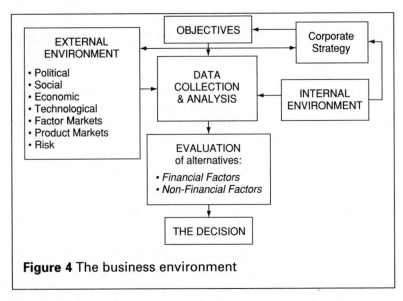

Figure 4 The business environment

It is of prime importance that the external environment is monitored on a regular basis. The early detection of change means that earlier corrective action can be taken.

The concepts

Profit and loss accounts and balance sheets are prepared using money measurement, i.e. only items which can be measured in monetary terms are shown. Thus, critical success factors such as good industrial relations, morale and the calibre and ability of the management are not shown. Some texts make a distinction between accounting concepts, principles and conventions. To simplify matters we will just call them all concepts. The following alphabetical list provides you with a brief explanation of how each concept is applied in practice:

- **Consistency** – accounts are prepared on a consistent basis from year to year, for example, using the same accounting policies for the valuation of stocks and work in progress, and the treatment of depreciation, the translation of foreign currencies, and so on.
- **Disclosure** – matters which have a significant impact on the figures reported in the published accounts should be disclosed. For example, where it has been necessary to change an accounting policy, post-balance sheet events.
- **Entity** – the accounts are prepared for the business entity, for example, a company is classed as a separate legal individual. The personal transactions of the owners should be kept separate.
- **Fairness** – the accounts need to give a true and fair view.
- **Going concern** – assumes that the business is going to continue and values assets and liabilities accordingly, as opposed to a 'winding up basis' in which case the assets and liabilities would be valued at their 'break up values'.
- **Matching (accruals)** – charges expenses in the period in which the sales revenue to which they relate is reported, or to the period in which the expense is consumed. For example the value of closing stock at the end of the period will be charged in the period in which the stock is sold. Expenditure such as lighting and heating charges for the current financial year should be charged as an expense for that year even though it has not yet been paid. The opposite of an accrual is a prepayment, i.e. something paid out in the current period such as rent or insurance of buildings, the benefit of which extends into the next financial year.
- **Materiality** – helps to determine whether to charge expenditure to the profit and loss account or to carry it forward into the future as an asset in the balance sheet. The judgement rests on whether or not the item in question is significant in terms of value. What is a significant value will depend upon the size of the company and the person making the judgement.

- **Objectivity** – personal bias has to be eliminated when preparing the financial statements.
- **Prudence (Conservatism)** – this reflects the conservative image which is sometimes portrayed by accountants. The way in which prudence is applied can be described as: do not anticipate profit and provide for all possible losses. This means that accountants tend to understate profits. A lot of the profits which are calculated and reported nowadays are influenced by what is and what is not allowable for tax purposes.
- **Cost concept** – items such as fixed assets are shown at their historic cost or at their historic cost less depreciation in the balance sheet. What we actually paid for an asset is a matter of fact. Assets, can however, be re-valued to reflect significant changes in their value, for example, freehold land and buildings, and stocks of raw materials.
- **Realization** – determines when a credit sale is to be included in the sales figure in the profit and loss account (for income measurement purposes). In the profit and loss account the sales figure should include all of the cash and credit sales for the period.

Accounting is not an exact science and depends upon the judgement of those individuals who prepare the accounts and the way in which they apply the concepts. The tax factor can affect reported profits.

The role of IT

The recording systems for the smallest to the largest companies/organizations can be handled via computers with the information stored on the hard drive and/or discs. The books of account, for example, analysed cash books, ledgers, day books, and so on can all be stored in this form. Numerous software packages can produce accounts, credit control information, payroll, statistics, budgets, net present value calculations, and so on. File security is important in such systems and back up copies need to be kept in case of a disaster. The output from the system, however, still needs to take into account the needs of the user.

KEY WORDS	
Financial accounting	Cost and management accounting
Financial management	Financial recording system
Credit control	Historic – statutory report and
Pre-determined information	accounts
Financing decisions	Investment decisions
Companies Act 1985 and 1989	Profitability
Auditors' report	Liquidity

Further reading

Atrill P. and McLaney E., Chapter 1 *Accounting and Finance for Non-specialists*, Prentice Hall, 1997.

Chadwick L., Chapter 1 *Essential Financial Accounting for Managers*, Financial Times Prentice Hall, 2001.

You may find the following text useful throughout your studies:

Wood F. & Sangster A., *Frank Wood's A-Level Accounting*, Financial Times Prentice Hall, 1998.

Useful websites

You may find the following web sites useful throughout your studies:

A/AS Level Accounting

www.ocr.org.uk/develop/ACCOUNT/accounta.htm

The Virtual School of Accounting and Finance

WWW.ITBP.COM

Support for users of the Frank Wood books, for example, exam tips, multiple-choice questions, tutorial support books, and so on:

www.booksites.net/wood

Essay topics

1. Explain the principal differences between financial accounting, cost and management accounting and financial management. [25 marks]

2. 'The application of the accounting concepts may have a significant affect on reported profits and losses and the valuation of assets'. Discuss this statement. [25 marks]

Chapter Two

Sources of business finance

'Finance is an extremely scarce and expensive commodity and should be used in exactly the same way as any other scarce resource, that is, with efficiency.' Leslie Chadwick

Costs and risks

Financing has been described on many occasions as a **system of costs and risks**. If the borrower is high risk they have to pay more for their money, if they are low risk they have to pay less for their money. Finance is always available to anyone, but at a price! This means that the very successful companies which have sound financial performance records, lots of assets and impressive future plans will be able to attract finance at a much lower cost than say, a new company which has not yet proved itself in terms of financial performance and as yet does not own a lot of assets.

The risk may be reduced to the lender which in turn reduces the cost to the borrower in cases where the borrower is able to pledge **security**, for example, lending such as secured loans and overdrafts. The security may be by a **fixed charge** (pledging specific assets such as land and buildings or machinery or equipment) or a **floating charge** (a general charge over all the assets). In the event of default by the borrower, the lender would, subject to pre-preferential claims, be able to sell the assets in question to satisfy their debt.

External sources of business finance

Finance is needed for financing long-term, medium-term and short-term investments. The definition of each depends to a large extent on the size of the company and the nature of the industry. For example long-term could mean twenty years in the aviation industry, fifteen years in the car industry and ten years in certain manufacturing industries.

Major sources of long-term finance

Ordinary share capital

The ordinary shareholders, in most cases, have **voting rights** and so can determine who has **control** of the company. Certain companies, for example, those which are owned by a small number of shareholders, may not wish to issue lots of shares to the public because this could lead to a loss of control. The price at which a share is issued is made up of its **par** or **face** (or nominal) **value**, for example, £1 per share, and the **share premium** (the amount which will be received over and above the par value). Therefore, £1 shares issued for £2.75 would have a share premium of £1.75 per share. The total amount to be received per share could be made up of so much on application, so much on being allotted the shares and the remainder via one or more instalments (the instalments to be received at a future date are termed **calls**). The ordinary shareholder's reward for investing in the company is twofold, **dividends**, and **capital gains** (or **capital losses**). They do bear the greatest risk, in that they get paid out last if the company goes into liquidation or becomes bankrupt. The value of shares which are quoted on the Stock Exchange are affected by supply and demand for the shares, growth, earnings, dividends, financial performance and **market expectations**.

Mini-case: ASDA

Several years ago the ASDA share price was very low. The company had lost its way. My advice at the time was buy their shares. The best time to buy shares is when the price is low and before the price goes up. It is, however, a risk as the price may continue to fall. Over the period which followed the share price more than doubled!
What were my reasons for suggesting the purchase of their shares?

Answer
I believed at the time that they were vulnerable to a take-over and that this would cause a dramatic increase in the share price. As it happened, they did a fantastic turn-around and the share price more than doubled! Years later they were taken over by another company.

If the ordinary shareholders want their money back they can sell their shares. Note that the ordinary shareholders may be described as the **equity shareholders**.

Preference shares

The **preference shares** tend to have a fixed dividend and no votes unless their dividend is owing. In a winding up they get paid out before the ordinary shareholders. There are many different types of preference shares, for example, redeemable preference shares.

Long-term debt (or debt financing)
This is made up of debentures and long-term loans.

- **Debentures** are a special type of long-term loan. They are usually secured and carry a fixed rate of interest. The debenture holders are protected by a **deed of trust**. This will specify the earliest and latest dates on which the debenture holders will be repaid, and the actions of the trustees in the event of default, for example, if the company defaults in the payment of interest to its debenture holders, the trustees will petition the court to start legal proceedings to have the company wound up. In times of very poor trading conditions those companies which have a lot of debenture finance are the most likely to go out of business. They have to pay the interest to the debenture holders whether or not they make a profit.
- Long-term loans can be for various periods of time at either fixed or variable interest rates, secured or unsecured. They do not pose quite as much risk as debentures because it may be possible to arrange with the provider, for example, the bank, to re-schedule the debt repayments. They do, however, sometimes come with strings attached, for example, providing the lender with periodic accounts/cash flow forecasts and/or having to gain the lender's approval for investment plans. There are several different types of loans, such as start-up loans, loans with repayment holidays (for example, no repayments for the first two years, then repay at a higher rate), syndicated loans (for example, several banks joining together to spread the risk and provide a multi-million pound loan), government backed loan schemes, European Union loans etc.

Convertible loan stock or convertible debentures (convertibles)
Very successful companies with sound financial performance records and lots of assets should be able to issue convertibles. Other companies, for example, those who do not have such good financial performance records and not so many assets, could find it almost impossible to issue convertibles.

Convertibles tend to be fixed interest and the holders have an option to convert into ordinary shares at/from a specified future date. If the interest on their convertibles is much higher than the going rate they may decide not to convert and would just carry on receiving the interest until they do decide to convert.

The advantages to the company are that they never have to repay the capital, and at the time of issue the interest tends to be lower than say loans or debentures because of the conversion option. The only way the holders can get their money back is to convert into ordinary shares and then sell them to a third party. A **dilution of earnings** may take place if/when all the holders convert, leading to a lower earnings per share (the dilution effect) figure. Simply put, it creates a bigger earnings cake shared up between more ordinary shareholders so that they all end up with a smaller piece!

Leasing for the long-term

For example as in the case of Leasehold Land and Buildings. The definition of a short-lease is a lease for a period of up to 50 years. Thus, even a short-lease can be a long-term asset.

Sale and leaseback

This usually involves selling a fixed asset such as land and buildings to a financial institution such as an insurance company and then leasing it back. This will provide a lump sum to finance other projects.

Mini-case: To build, build and build

A local authority in England decided to build a new state of the art civic centre. Having completed the first part, an office block and car park, it then sold it to an insurance company for a considerable sum, and leased it back at an agreed annual rental figure. The sum received was then used to finance the next stage of the civic centre development .

The above could go on and on, selling, leasing back and building more and more. One of the possible downsides to the sale and leaseback system of raising finance is that at the end of a specified period there could be a rent review and the rent could go up by a significant amount.

Major sources of medium-term finance

Leasing

Leasing of assets for medium-term periods, for example, machinery, equipment, and computer hardware and so on. The financing of assets in this way means that they do not show up in the company's balance sheet.

This is described as '**off-balance-sheet**' financing. Some of the advantages claimed for this type of financing are:

- the company/organization does not have to find a lump sum
- the amounts paid under the terms of the lease each year will be charged as an expense in the profit and loss account
- such payments are usually allowed as deductions in computing taxable income (in the UK)
- if, because of advances in technology, it becomes necessary to replace a fixed asset such as computer hardware or other equipment, it may be possible to change more quickly where the assets have been leased. It can take a considerable amount of time to sell a fixed asset which has been bought outright.
- the effects on cash flow and profits are known. This makes planning for the future much easier and the forecasts more reliable
- the 'off-balance-sheet financing effect'. This causes the capital employed figure to be lower when compared with companies who purchase all of their fixed assets (see Chapter 6).

Hire purchase

This can be available to finance the purchase of assets in the medium-term. Some texts say that **hire purchase** (HP) is expensive. This is not always the case, due to increased competition between the providers.

Other medium-term sources include: loans, venture capital, government and EU funding and mortgage finance.

Major sources of short-term finance

Bank overdraft

This is often described as 'being repayable on demand'. Banks, however, only tend to call in an overdraft as a last resort, for example, where they can see no possibility of getting any of their money back unless they take immediate action.

Nowadays, some corporate customers do use their overdraft as a long-term source of funds, for example, an overdraft of an individual company which is secured on the assets of the whole group of companies.

Short-term loans

From banks, venture capitalists, government sources and so on.

Leasing

Of fixed assets such as motor vehicles.

Creditors (trade credit)

For goods and services on credit, these are a source of short-term finance, for example, 60 days before payment becomes due.

Mini-case: How to become a millionaire

Several years ago, Honest Ed, a Canadian supermarket owner, arranged for some of his suppliers to supply goods to him on 90 days credit. Within a very short space of time he sold the goods for cash. He was then able to invest the cash short-term until the payment date arrived and earn interest on it. This is known as the **treasury function**, i.e. the function in a business which invests surplus cash short-term. He became a millionaire, came to London and bought the *Old Vic* theatre in 1983.

Other creditors where there is a lead time between a debt being recognized and the cash being paid over include proposed dividends and tax outstanding.

Factoring/invoice discounting companies

These can, for a fee, make an advance of a certain percentage of a company's debtors (accounts receivable) for example from 75% to 85% of the client company's invoices. They may or may not take on the task of collecting the debts which are outstanding.

Bills of exchange

These are a promise to pay. They are drawn up by the seller who gets the purchaser to sign it (to signify that they accept it), and then return it to the seller. The seller can then discount the bill (i.e. receive payment, for a fee), at a bank, accepting house or discount house.

Alternative ways of financing assets

In addition to leasing, fixed assets can also be **rented** or hired, for example, office equipment, cleaning equipment, freezers, and so on. Again, these represent 'off-balance-sheet financing'.

One alternative to manufacturing a product or performing a service is to use **sub-contractors,** or to buy certain components from outside suppliers. This frees the company/organization from having to acquire more fixed assets such as premises and equipment, and current assets such as raw materials.

Internal sources of business finance

In addition to the external sources of finance, there are also some internal sources.

Retained earnings

The self-generated finance, **retained earnings** (this may also be described as retained profits, undistributed profits, profit and loss account balance or **ploughed back profits**) is one of the most important sources of business finance. It represents the accumulated profits which have been ploughed back and re-invested in the business.

Surplus assets

Companies/organizations may have some assets which are surplus to requirements. If these assets can be identified and disposed of it can generate additional cash flow. It could also bring about further savings. Disposing of fixed assets such as machinery and equipment, and current assets such as stocks of raw materials could free valuable space which could be used for other purposes. Surplus buildings could be sold off. Space no longer needed could be sub-let. There could also be savings in overheads, for example, lighting, heating, insurance and other costs associated with the holding of stocks (holding costs).

Efficiency

If the control of debtors – credit control – and the control of stocks of raw materials, work-in-progress, finished goods, and so on – stock control (inventory control) – are efficient, cash flow can be improved. This would mean less finance (capital) tied up in the working capital and make better use of existing funds.

Factors affecting the financing decision

Which type of finance should we use?

There are quite a number of factors which affect the choice of which type of finance to go for when a company/organization is in need of some additional finance, some of which are as follows:

Gearing The level of long-term debt (long-term loans and debentures) to equity (the issued ordinary share capital plus reserves). For example, if the company is highly geared, i.e. it has a high level of long-term debt compared to the equity, it may not be a good idea to try to obtain more long-term debt, as the market may not want to provide more long-term debt.

Security and asset cover Using fixed assets as security does mean lower cost finance.

Control To issue more equity, i.e. ordinary shares, could lead to a loss of control. This may cause, for example, a family-owned company or a company owned by a small number of shareholders not to issue any more.

Track record A sound financial performance record does open up more possibilities for raising finance, for example, convertible loan stock.

Cost The cost of the finance, for example, the interest payable and the fees such as set up costs. The taxation implications would also need to be considered.

Dividend policy The amount paid out as dividends does affect the amount which can be ploughed back and re-invested in the business.

Relationships The establishment of good working relationships with the providers of finance, for example, banks, venture capitalists and other financial institutions, can help when the company/organization is wanting to raise more finance.

Life cycle The position of the company/organization can help explain why they finance themselves in particular ways. For example, a company which is short of cash and lots of growth, will tend to have a very low dividend payout and a very high plough back.

Searching Shopping around for an appropriate offering, for example, a loan with a repayment holiday or hire purchase finance.

Term Is it needed for the long-, medium- or short-term?

Strings attached What conditions will have to be met? For example, where the provider has to vet future investment plans and/or providing cash flow forecasts at quarterly intervals.

Cost/benefit The cost of the finance, for example, in terms of any fees payable and interest costs, should not exceed the benefit to be derived from the investment of the funds acquired.

Financial plans

Financial plans aim at ensuring that the **corporate objectives**, for example, profit targets, market share, and so on, are achieved. The plans will need to be drawn up to cover the short-, medium- and long-term. They depend upon the forecasting which involves making assumptions about and the business environment, for example, in terms of growth, the rate of inflation, and so on.

The plans will no doubt include various targets/budgets, for example: cash flow forecasts (cash budgets); capital expenditure budgets; budgeted profit and loss accounts; budgeted balance sheets, and so on. They should also plan for the unexpected and try to answer the question, 'What happens if things go wrong?'

KEY WORDS

System of costs and risks	Security (secured, unsecured)
Ordinary share capital	Fixed or floating charge
Voting rights	Control
Par or face value	Share premium
Calls	Dividends
Capital gains (or losses)	Market expectations
Preference shares	Long-term loans
Debentures	Deed of trust
Convertible loan stock	Convertible debentures
Dilution of earnings	Leasing
Sale and leaseback	Off-balance-sheet financing
Hire purchase	Bank overdraft
Treasury function	Factoring and invoice
Bills of exchange	discounting
Renting	Sub-contractors
Retained earnings	Surplus assets
(ploughed back profits)	Gearing
Track record	Security and asset cover
Life cycle	Relationships
Cost/benefit	Strings attached
Corporate objectives	Financial plans

Further reading

Atrill P. & McLaney E., Chapter 12 *Accounting and Finance for Non-Specialists*, Financial Times Prentice Hall, 2001.

Davies D., Chapter 13 *The Art of Managing Finance*, McGraw-Hill, 1997.

Chadwick L. & Kirkby D., Chapters 3 and 4 *Financial Management*, Routledge, 1995.

Useful websites

These could be useful to you throughout your studies.

For the Atrill & McLaney website:

http://www.booksites.net/atrillmclaney

How to find out about Accounting, Banking and Financial Information:
www.hw.ac.uk/library/howtoaccounting.html
The latest accountancy news:
www.moreover.com/cgi-local/page?o=portal&c=Accounting%20news

Essay topics

1. The directors of a small company (turnover £2m), went along to see their bank manager about either increasing their overdraft limit or taking out a term loan for a period of 10 years. When confronted by them, the bank manager said, 'Why should we, the bank, risk all our money if you are not prepared to risk your own money?'
   a. Discuss the pros and cons of the directors' financing proposals. [10 marks]
   b. Comment on the attitude taken by the bank manager and the possible ways in which the directors could take over some of the risk or satisfy the bank manager. [15 marks]

2. Financing has been described as 'a system of costs and risks'. Discuss and illustrate this statement, and in doing so show how the company's position in its life cycle will affect its ability to raise finance. [25 marks]

Data response question

1. Study the information and answer **all** parts of the question which follows.

VITALITY plc

The following information relates to Vitality plc, an international food business marketing a long-established range of biscuits, snacks, chocolate bars and frozen products. A new range of products aimed towards healthier eating is being planned for the year 20X8. A sum of £70 million will be required to cover all the costs of the launch. It has always been company policy to increase the dividend paid per share each year but the chairman wants this policy reviewed at the next board meeting.

The company accountant holds the view that brand names should be included in the accounts to give a true and fair view.

VITALITY plc: FINANCIAL HIGHLIGHTS

	20X6	20X5	20X4
Profit after tax	£18 million	£21 million	£30 million
Dividend cover	1.2 times	1.5 times	2.5 times
Dividend per share	10 pence	9.3 pence	8 pence

VITALITY plc: Balance Sheet as at 31 December 20X6

	£m	£m
Fixed assets		650
Current assets		
Stock	110	
Debtors	200	
Cash	50	360
Current liabilities		305
Net current assets		55
Assets employed		705
Financed by:		
Long-term loan	200	
Share capital	415	
Profit and loss account reserves	90	
Capital employed		705

Adapted from AQA Q2, Paper 5, Summer 2000

(a) With reference to the data, explain how the £70 million needed to launch the new product range could be raised from internal sources of finance. [6 marks]

 (b) Consider the accountant's view that the value of Vitality's leading biscuit and chocolate brand names should be included in the balance sheet to give 'a true and fair view' (line 8) of the accounts. [6 marks]

 (c) Evaluate the company policy of increasing the dividend per share to investors each year. [9 marks]

Chapter Three

The final accounts of companies (part 1)

'Accounting is something that affects people in their personal lives just as much as it affects very large businesses.'
Wood F. & Sangster A., *Business Accounting 1*, Financial Times Prentice Hall, 1999.

'When asked by a client to prepare their final accounts for them, the accountant replied, "Yes, I can do that, would you like to end up with a profit or a loss?"'
Anonymous

Introduction

Students, managers, executives, government ministers, teachers and members of the public at large who are non-accountants, quite frequently have numerous questions concerning the final accounts of companies. Accounting has been described as 'the language of business'; however, the terminology which is used is horrific and the financial statements which are produced are extremely difficult to comprehend. Some of the typical questions and comments made relating to the final accounts are as follows:

- What are the final accounts?
- What is a profit and loss account?
- What is a balance sheet?
- I know that when people talk about the bottom line that they are talking about the profit or loss, but how is it arrived at?
- The company report is really very interesting until you come into contact with the accounting information. It then becomes a minefield!

The three key financial statements

The three key financial statements are:

1. the profit and loss account
2. the balance sheet
3. the cash flow statement.

Together, they may be described as the **final accounts**. They are the end product of the accounting recording system, a system which records the business transactions in the books of account.

The profit and loss account

This helps to answer the question, 'How much profit have we made for the period?' The profit and loss account can also be described as the income statement or the P & L. The way in which the profit or loss is computed depends upon the application of the accounting concepts and the accounting policies which are adopted.

As mentioned earlier in this text, the tax factor can and does affect the way in which the profit or loss is calculated, and in particular the application of the realization concept, the materiality concept, the prudence concept and the distinction between capital and **revenue expenditure**.

Mini-case: The 'cut off'

When companies such as manufacturing companies are getting near to their year end they decide on a cut-off date. After this date any goods coming in will not be included in stock, creditors and purchases, and any items going out will not be deducted from stock and not be included in debtors and sales.

This means that any profit earned between the **cut-off date** and the year end will not be included until the following year. The amount of profit earned in this period can vary significantly from year to year. The way in which the cut-off period is managed can cause errors which in turn affect the reported profits or losses. For example, goods may be included in stock but excluded from the purchases and creditors. The profit and loss account has four sections which are as illustrated in Figure 5.

The profit and loss account

1. The trading account section
2. Non-trading income section
3. The profit and loss account section
4. The appropriation account section

Figure 5 The four component parts of the profit and loss account

---

All four component parts run into each other and merge to form the profit and loss account.

The trading account section

The main purpose of the trading account is to calculate the **gross profit**. In its most simple form this can be:

Sales less the cost of sales = gross profit.

Where the cost of sales is computed:

opening stock add purchases *(this gives the total value of stock which is available for resale)*, less the closing stock.

What is included in the cost of sales does depend on the nature of the business. For example:

- **A manufacturing company** could include all the direct costs of manufacture. This could include stocks of raw materials and work-in-progress, the raw materials purchased, carriage charges on the raw materials purchased, the cost of the labour used in manufacture; and factory overheads such as rent, light and heat, cleaners' wages; and also the depreciation of machinery.
- **A firm of management consultants** could include all the direct costs of providing the service, for example, consultants' salaries, travelling expenses, software, stationery, and so on.
- **A road haulage company** could include drivers' wages, vehicle running costs, ferry charges, vehicle cleaning, and so on.

Non-trading income

This will be added on to the **gross profit**, and could include: investment income, for example, dividends received as a result of owning shares in other companies; rent received from letting property; and discount received for paying amounts owing to creditors promptly.

The profit and loss account section

All of the expenses for the period, for example, administration expenses, selling and distribution expenses, bank interest and charges, loan interest, debenture interest, directors' salaries, light and heat, rent of fixed assets, hire purchase interest, legal and professional fees, depreciation of fixed assets, and so on will be deducted from the gross profit to arrive at the **net profit before tax**. You should observe that the net profit before tax is the figure which remains after charging directors' fees and salaries, and also after charging loan and debenture interest.

THE APPROPRIATION SECTION
(appropriation account)

	£000	£000
Net profit before tax		72,000
Less tax		32,000
Net profit after tax		40,000
Less appropriations:		
Transfer to general reserve	15,000	
Preference share dividends	2,000	
Paid and proposed dividends on		
Ordinary shares	5,000	22,000
Retained earnings this year		18,000
Add retained earnings brought forward		106,000
RETAINED EARNINGS carried forward		124,000

Figure 6 A typical appropriation account

The appropriation section

This section shows how the net profit before tax is shared up between the interested parties and how much is being ploughed back and retained by the company. Figure 6 provides you with a specimen format and should help you to follow the calculations which are involved.

You should note that loan interest and debenture interest are *not* appropriations and have been dealt with in calculating the net profit before tax. The £15m transferred to the General Reserve still represents ploughed back profits. Preference **dividends**, if any, are classed as appropriations. Note also that the amount which is included for ordinary share dividends is the amount which has already been paid for the year (the interim dividend) if any, and the proposed final dividend for the year.

The amount of retained earnings which has been brought forward from the previous year of £106m represents the cumulative retained earnings which has been ploughed back and reinvested by the company since its formation. The £124m retained earnings includes the current year's plough back and is the figure which will appear in the current year's balance sheet under the heading of **retained earnings** (or *Profit & Loss Account Balance*, or *Undistributed Profits*).

You should note that the profit and loss account of Greenhead Scientific Supplies PLC in Figure 7 is in summary format and for internal reporting purposes. Note also that when we talk about the **operating profit**, that this is the profit from trading operations and before interest payments and other non-trading expenses and non-trading income (if any). When the

GREENHEAD SCIENTIFIC SUPPLIES PLC

Profit and loss account for the year ended 31st December, 20X4

	20X4 £million	20X3 £million
Net sales	3,218	1,867
Less Cost of sales	2,350	1,364
GROSS PROFIT	868	503
Less Expenses:		
Selling, distribution, administration, research and development etc.	726	434
OPERATING PROFIT	142	69
Less Interest paid	41	20
NET PROFIT BEFORE TAX	101	49
Less Corporation tax	47	23
NET PROFIT AFTER TAX	54	26
Less Dividend paid	2	2
RETAINED PROFIT	52	24
Add Profit and loss balance brought forward	38	14
PROFIT AND LOSS ACCOUNT BALANCE	90	38

Figure 7 A profit and loss account in summary format

final accounts are prepared for internal purposes it is usual to provide **corresponding figures** for the year before (or the last few years). In our example there were no transfers to **reserves** in the appropriation section. Finally you should appreciate that the figure of £90m, described as the profit and loss account balance, is the cumulative retained earnings figure which will be shown in the reserves section of the balance sheet in Figure 9 below.

The balance sheet

The balance sheet may be described as a **position statement**, in that it shows the financial position of the company at a specific point in time. It is in fact rather like a photograph. Take the picture today, and you see a picture of health. Take the picture tomorrow or next week or next month, and the picture could have changed quite dramatically.

The balance sheet may also be described as a statement of assets and liabilities. It shows where the money (capital, finance) came from and how

---

BALANCE SHEET AS AT 31 DECEMBER, 20X8

EMPLOYMENT OF CAPITAL (USES):

Fixed Assets plus Investments plus Working Capital

CAPTAL EMPLOYED (SOURCES):

Share Capital plus Reserves plus Long-term Debt (Loans)

Figure 8 The structure of a balance sheet (for internal purposes)

---

it has been invested. The **cost concept** tends to be the principal method which is used to value the assets. The fixed assets may be valued at their historic cost or historic cost less depreciation. They may also be re-valued. The stocks/inventory may be shown at the lower of cost or **net realizable value** (i.e. what they could be sold for). Figure 8 provides you with a quick overview of the structure of a balance sheet which has been drawn up for internal reporting purposes.

The fixed assets

Those assets acquired for use in the business over a long period of time and which are not for re-sale are called fixed assets. They consist of: freehold and leasehold land and buildings; plant, machinery and equipment; furniture, fixtures and fittings; and motor vehicles, and so on. Other than leasehold land and buildings (property), fixed assets which are leased or rented are not included with the fixed assets in the balance sheet. You may recall that earlier we referred to them as '**off-balance-sheet financing**'.

In addition, we can also have **intangible assets**, for example, patents, trademarks, brand names and goodwill, and so on. You can't see them, but they are there, and do have a value.

Investments

Quoted and unquoted investments in other companies/government stocks are included under this heading.

The **working capital** is the figure which some describe as the **net current assets**, and it is calculated as follows:

Working Capital = Current Assets less Current Liabilities

It includes the short-term circulating capital which is used to finance the everyday operating type expenses. For example, short-term finance is provided by those who supply goods and services on credit (the creditors),

sales are made on credit to customers (debtors) and for cash, the cash received is used to pay the labour force and expenses, and so on.

The current assets are made up of stocks and inventory, debtors, pre-paid expenses, short-term investments, bank balances and cash balances.

The **current liabilities** (debts which will have to be paid within the next twelve months), include creditors, expenses which are owing (accrued expenses or accruals), tax owing, proposed dividends owing to the share-holders, and so on.

The **share capital** could be made up of the issued **ordinary share capital** (the amount called up or fully paid up) and the issued **preference share capital**.

Reserves

The reserves belong to the ordinary shareholders and may be divided up as follows:

- **Capital reserves** – reserves which are not distributable as dividends, for example, a revaluation reserve which comes into being on the revaluation of certain fixed assets.
- **Share premium account** – the amount received from an issue of shares which is over and above the par (or face or nominal) value. This can only be used for certain purposes laid down by the Companies Acts 1985 and 1989, for example, to provide the premium on the redemption of debentures.
- **General reserves** – As mentioned earlier, these are just the cumulative ploughed back profits which are described under another name, rather than being included under the heading of retained earnings.

The **long-term debt** can be made up of long-term loans and/or debentures You should now be able to see how all this comes together by working through the example balance sheet which is illustrated in Figure 9.
From your review of the balance sheet of Greenhead Scientific Supplies Plc you should again note that corresponding figures for 20X3 have been provided. You should have also noticed the following:

The employment of capital

This shows how the capital invested in the business has been used and how it is represented at the balance sheet date, for example, used to buy fixed assets and tied up in current assets with some short-term financing coming via the current liabilities.

GREENHEAD SCIENTIFIC SUPPLIES PLC

Balance Sheet as at 31 December 20X4

THE EMPLOYMENT OF CAPITAL

	20X4	20X3
FIXED ASSETS	£million	£million
Freehold land and buildings (net book value)	350	300
Equipment, fixtures and fittings	280	242
	630	542
CURRENT ASSETS		
Stock/Inventories	150	65
Debtors/Receivables	236	142
Marketable securities	32	40
Cash and bank balances	12	19
	430	266

CURRENT LIABILITIES (*Creditors falling due within the next twelve months*)

Creditors/Accounts payable	110	90
Accrued expenses	53	37
Taxation	47	23
Proposed dividend	2	2
	212	152

WORKING CAPITAL (*Net current assets, i.e.* *Current assets less Current liabilities*)	218	114
	848	656

Authorized Share Capital	200 million £1 Ordinary Shares

CAPITAL EMPLOYED

	£million	£million
ISSUED SHARE CAPITAL		
Ordinary share capital (£1 per share)	120	120
RESERVES		
Share premium	66	50
Profit and loss account (retained earnings)	90	38
Ordinary shareholders funds (equity)	276	208
LONG-TERM DEBT		
Long-term loans and debentures	572	448
	848	656

Figure 9 The balance sheet of a company

Fixed assets
We only had two categories of fixed assets. There could have been others depending on the type of business, for example, leasehold premises, machinery and so on. The company did not have any intangible assets or investments other than the short-term investments (marketable securities).

Current assets
These are shown in the order of liquidity, i.e. the order in which they can be converted into cash. The marketable securities are shown as current assets and represent short-term investments which are held to be readily realizable so as to provide an injection of cash when needed.

Current liabilities
Current liabilities represent creditors and amounts owing which it is estimated will be settled and paid off within the next twelve months.

Working capital
The working capital (also called the net current assets), is simply the difference between the current assets and the current liabilities. Working capital management is concerned with the control and management of stocks, debtors, short-term investments, cash and creditors.

Capital employed
This shows where the money which has been invested in the company has come from, for example, ordinary shares, share premium, retained earnings and long-term debt.

Authorized share capital
The authorized share capital statement is included for information purposes. The authorized share capital is the maximum amount of share capital that the company can issue.

Issued share capital
Shows the amount of the par or face value per share which has been received to date.

Reserves
The **share premium** is the amount received from the issue of the ordinary shares which is over and above the par or face value of the shares, an extra £16m came in during year 20X4. This company did not have a capital reserve or a general reserve. The profit and loss account (retained

earnings) heading describes the cumulative profits which have been ploughed back to date and reinvested in the company.

Ordinary shareholders funds (equity)
Is exactly what it says. The amount which has been invested in the company by/on behalf of the ordinary shareholders, i.e. ordinary share capital plus reserves.

Long-term debt (long-term liabilities)
The long-term finance other than shares which has been loaned to the company, for example, long-term loans and debentures.

Cash flow statements
The **cash flow statement** shows where all the cash came from over the accounting period – profits, more share capital, new loans etc. – and how it has been used, for example, to buy new fixed assets, to pay dividends and tax, and so on. It is a historic statement i.e. it looks back at the past. Do not confuse it with the cash flow forecast (i.e. the cash budget), this looks at the future. We will study the composition of this statement in greater depth in Chapter 5.

Capital or revenue expenditure
Capital expenditure is the amount spent on purchasing fixed assets such as premises, machinery, equipment, office furniture, and so on. The items in question will be capitalized. This means that they will be carried forward into future accounting periods in the balance sheet as fixed assets. The assets concerned are long-term assets.

Revenue expenditure is the description which is applied to the various items of expenditure which have to be charged in the profit and loss account in computing the net profit before tax, for example, wages and salaries of employees, materials used to produce the goods and services, overhead expenses.

Depreciation of fixed assets
The aim of depreciation is to spread the cost of the fixed asset over its useful life. The expenditure on the fixed asset is in effect used up and consumed over several years. Two of the main methods which are used quite extensively are: the straight line method and the reducing balance method.

The straight line method

The **straight line method** charges the same amount in the profit and loss account for depreciation each year/period, for example, using a percentage of cost or a percentage of cost less residual value.

Mini-case: What should we do?

Wang Ying Trading Co. Ltd purchased equipment on 1 April 20X7 for £270,000. Their next year end is on 30 June, 2X07. They have asked you to suggest how much they should charge in their accounts for depreciation. In order to do this you needed to obtain answers to a number of questions. The questions and answers to those questions were as follows:

- How long will the equipment be used within the company? Answer 5 years.
- Will the equipment have a scrap or residual value at the end of 5 years? Answer £20,000.

We will now use this information for demonstrating how the straight line method of dealing with depreciation works.

STRAIGHT LINE METHOD OF DEPRECIATION

$$\frac{\text{Cost less residual value}}{\text{Life}} \qquad \frac{\text{£270,000 less £20,000}}{\text{5 years}} \qquad = \text{£50,000 per year}$$

The way in which this would be shown in the balance sheet each year would be:

Fixed Assets (£000)	Cost	Depreciation	Net to date
Year 1 Equipment	270	50	220
Year 2 Equipment	270	100	170

At the end of Year 5 the net book value (net) would be equal to the residual value of £20,000. You should note that in the balance sheet it is usual to show the cost of the fixed asset less the cumulative depreciation to date in order to arrive at the net book value (net). Note also that the method illustrated charges a full year's depreciation in the year of purchase (in the above case they had only acquired the equipment just three months before the year end) and would not charge any depreciation for the year in which the fixed asset is sold/disposed of.

Both the straight line method and the **reducing balance method** can charge depreciation from the date of purchase to the date of sale on a **time apportionment** basis. For example, in our illustration only one quarter of a year's depreciation would be charged in Year 1, i.e. £12,500.

It is common practice in many companies to ignore the residual value. One of the reasons for this is that it is difficult to estimate what the figure will be. Had this been the case in the above example, the straight line depreciation figure per year would have been £270,000 divided by 5 = £54,000.

The reducing balance method

This method charges the selected percentage of the cost in the first year and then as a percentage of the net book value (net) from the second year onwards.

Mini-case: When we come to sell the fixed asset

Vic-bekum Plc purchased state of the art office furniture and equipment in 20X4 for £500,000. Depreciation at the rate of 20% reducing balance method was considered to be appropriate. Changes in technology dictated that the whole lot had to be replaced in 20X7. The amount received for the trade-in and sale of the old office furniture and equipment was £60,000.

THE REDUCING BALANCE METHOD

The amounts charged in the profit and loss account each year would have been, as follows:

Year	Cost or net book value brought forward £000	Depreciation @ 20% £000	Net book value carried forward £000
20×4	500	100	400
20×5	400	80	320
20×6	320	64	256
20×7	256		
Less sale proceeds	60		
LOSS ON SALE	196		

In 20X7 the loss of £196,000 would be charged as an expense in the profit and loss account. An alternative way of describing the loss on sale is to call it an under provision of depreciation i.e. if enough depreciation had been charged the net book value of the asset would have been equal to the sale proceeds. Thus, profits or losses on the sale of fixed assets are in effect an adjustment of the depreciation charge. For example, if too much depreciation had been charged, the result would be a loss on sale, i.e., an over provision of depreciation. This amount would have to be added back in the profit and loss account.

The revaluation method

Another method worthy of a mention is the revaluation method. The depreciation charge for the period is simply, the difference between the value of the fixed asset at the start of the period compared with its value at the end of the period. It could be used for fixed assets such as hand tools.

KEY WORDS

Final accounts	Revenue expenditure
Cut-off date	Cost of sales
Gross profit	Net profit before tax
Appropriation section	Dividends
Retained earnings	Operating profit
Corresponding figures	Reserves
Position statement	Cost concept
Net realizable value	Off-balance-sheet financing
Intangible assets	Working capital
Net current assets	Current assets
Current liabilities	Ordinary share capital
Preference share capital	Long-term debt
Share premium	Ordinary shareholder funds
Equity	Capital employed
Cash flow statement	Capital expenditure
Depreciation of fixed assets	Straight line method
Reducing balance method	Time apportionment basis

Further reading

Burns, P. & Morris, P., *Business Finance, A Pictorial Guide*, Butterworth-Heinemann, 1994.

Chadwick, L., Chapters 4 & 5 *Essential Financial Accounting for Managers*, Financial Times Prentice Hall, 2001

Dyson, J., Chapter 6 *Accounting for Non-Accounting Students*, Financial Times Prentice Hall, 2001.

Useful websites

Dyson's website *(very useful)*
http://www.booksites.net/dyson
Depreciation
www.learn.co.uk/default.asp?WC1=Unit&WCU=3103

Essay topics

1. Describe briefly the purpose and composition of:
   - the profit and loss account [12 marks]
   - the balance sheet. [13 marks]

2. What would the effect be on the profit and loss account, and the balance sheet if it were decided **not** to charge any depreciation? [25 marks]

Chapter Four

The final accounts of companies (part 2)

'Several of our machines that have been written down to nil for account-ing purposes will remain in use for many years to come!'
'Our freehold land and buildings are included in our accounts at their 1962 purchase price.'
'The debtors figure is after deducting a provision for bad and doubtful debts.'
These are some of the typical comments that tend to be made concerning the valuation of assets.

The valuation of assets
The way in which assets are valued can have a significant impact on the profit and loss account and/or the balance sheet. The key information which relates to the valuation of assets in the *Annual Report and Accounts*, is the **statement of accounting policies**.

Fixed assets
The fixed assets, for example, premises, equipment, motor vehicles, may be shown at their historic cost or historic cost less depreciation. The fixed assets may be re-valued, in which case the depreciation charge would be based on the revaluation. You should note that any increase in the value of the fixed assets caused by a revaluation will **not** increase the profit in the profit and loss account. The reason for this is because it is not a **real-ized profit**. Profits are generated when goods and services have been sold, and the asset has not been sold and will not therefore result in an inflow of cash. The increase in value will be added to the fixed asset in question, and also added to a **capital reserve** (or revaluation reserve).

Mini-case: The revaluation of a fixed asset

The Summer Bay Co Ltd bought some freehold buildings several years ago for £6m. It has now been re-valued at £54m and will be shown at this amount in the next balance sheet. The effect on the profit and loss account would be nil, and the effect on the capital reserve in the balance sheet would be an increase of £48m (£54m less £6m).

The role of accounting standards and financial reporting standards

Accounting standards (SSAPs) and financial reporting standards (FRSs) provide the guidelines/recommendations on various matters including the valuation of assets, for example, accounting policies; stocks and long-term contracts; research and development; foreign currency translation; leases and hire purchase; goodwill and intangible assets etc. We will now continue to review the valuation of assets other than the fixed assets. In doing so, we will be following the recommendations of the relevant SSAPs and FRSs.

Research and development expenditure

Pure and applied research costs should be charged in the profit and loss account as an expense for the year in which they are incurred, i.e. they are **written off** as an expense. This follows the prudence concept in that the future benefits of the research are uncertain.

On the other hand, development costs, i.e. the work involved with the development of new or existing products or services, if the outcome can be predicted with reasonable certainty may be carried forward in the balance sheet and written off over the period which benefits from those costs. For example, £300,000 spent to prolong the life of an existing product for three years could be written off at the rate of £100,000 per year in the profit and loss account. It could be described as a *deferred expense*, i.e. something paid out now, but the benefit to be derived from the expense extends into the future.

Goodwill and intangibles

The principal objective of Financial Reporting Standard 10 (FRS 10) *Goodwill and Intangible Assets*, is to ensure that purchased goodwill and intangible assets are charged in the profit and loss account in the periods in which they are depleted.

Goodwill

Purchased **goodwill** is the difference between the cost of acquiring an entity, for example, a subsidiary company, and a fair value of the assets and liabilities which have been acquired. It is recommended that purchased goodwill be capitalized and shown as an asset on the balance sheet. It is also recommended that internally generated goodwill not be capitalized.

Intangibles

Intangible assets, i.e. assets which do not have a physical existence (you cannot see them and you cannot touch them), include: goodwill, licences, patents, copyrights and franchises, and so on. It is recommended that an intangible asset which is purchased separately from a business should be capitalized at its cost. In cases where the intangible is acquired at the time of acquiring another entity, it should be capitalized and shown separately from the purchased goodwill, if its value can be reliably ascertained.

Depreciation of goodwill and intangibles

Depreciation should be charged over their estimated useful lives. If the life of the intangible is regarded as being indefinite it should not be capitalized i.e. it will be charged as an expense in the profit and loss account.

Note that in FRS 10 there are also special provisions relating to situations where the estimated economic life is greater than 20 years, and other matters.

Investments

Investments which are considered to be of a long-term nature are shown as fixed assets. Those which are short-term, for example, marketable securities, which are held to be readily realizable are shown as current assets.

Those investments which are held as fixed assets need to be classified under various headings, for example, shares held in group companies, loans to group companies, and other shares etc. The other shares can be quoted or unquoted shares. Note that where the market value of the quoted shares differs from the value shown in the balance sheet, the market value must be disclosed.

Stocks and work in progress

Stocks of raw materials should be valued at the lower of cost or **net realizable value**. However, in practice, when stock taking is being carried out the net realizable value of certain items may not be known.

The value of work in progress and finished goods may be arrived at using various methods, for example, the pricing of the materials used could use FIFO (first in, first out), LIFO (last in, first out) or AVECO (average cost) plus the amount to be included for production overhead expenses and other overhead expenses. The key here tends to be consistency i.e. using the same method year after year.

Accounting policies

To conclude this section on the valuation of assets we will now look at a real live but edited extract which has been taken from the accounts of *AMEC 1999*.

Basis of accounting

The accounts have been prepared under the historical cost convention modified to include the revaluation of certain fixed assets.

Depreciation

Depreciation is provided on all tangible assets, other than freehold land, at the rates calculated to write off the cost or valuation, less estimated residual value, of each asset on a straight line basis over its estimated useful life, as follows:

Freehold buildings	50 years
Leasehold land and buildings	the shorter of the lease term or 50 years
Plant and equipment	mainly three to five years

Foreign currencies

Assets and liabilities denominated in foreign currencies are translated into sterling at the rate ruling at the balance sheet date. Trading results are translated at average rates for the year.

Goodwill

Goodwill arising on acquisitions post 1 January 1998 is capitalized and amortized (i.e. depreciated) over its estimated useful life.

Leases

Operating leases are charged to the profit and loss account in the year in which they are incurred.

Stocks

Stocks are stated at the lower of cost or net realizable value.

The importance of changing asset values

The value at which fixed assets are stated in the balance sheet is affected by the purchase and sale of fixed assets, the depreciation charged in the profit and loss account each year/period, and the revaluation of fixed assets.

The amount of depreciation charged does affect the net profit before tax and the amount carried forward into the future as retained earnings.

Note, however, that in the UK the amount charged in the financial accounts in the majority of cases is **not** the same as the amount which is allowed for tax purposes. The tax authorities in the UK have their own system of depreciation called capital allowances.

When fixed assets are **re-valued** upwards, this increases the amount of capital employed in the company. As mentioned earlier, the increase brought about by a revaluation will not affect the profit and loss account. Profits could in fact go down because the deprecation charge (if any), would be based on the re-valued value of the fixed asset. This would mean that the ratio of profit to capital employed would go down (return on capital employed). We would be expressing the same or a lower profit figure over a higher capital employed figure.

Fixed assets can be used as security to obtain lower cost financing, such as long-term loans and/or debentures. Including them at more realistic values in the balance sheet should provide a better indication of the security available to attract **secured lending**. It would also give a fairer picture of the worth of the company.

Writing amounts off stocks and debtors will reduce profits/retained earnings and the amount of capital employed. For example, writing £25,000 off stocks would reduce the profit before tax and the retained earnings by that amount, and the stock value would have been reduced by £25,000. The overall effect would be a reduction in the capital employed of £25,000. The value assigned to stock and debtors will affect some of the ratios, for example, current assets to current liabilities, stock to turnover (sales), debtor days. We will make a more in-depth review of these and other ratios in Chapter 6.

Investments shown at their cost could still have a note of their market value included in the information. This means that the information is more up to date and more realistic for assessing how much the company is worth.

The amendment and modification of the final accounts

How will an error, or alternative treatment of a transaction, or a change made to an accounting policy affect the final accounts? The quick answer is, most of the errors which occur will tend to affect the final accounts.

The impact of errors

To illustrate the impact which errors have on the final accounts we will look at a selection of those errors which may occur more frequently. Firstly, you should note that errors made before the preparation of the final accounts should be found when the **trial balance** is prepared (a trial balance is extracted to ensure that the accounts are in balance before the preparation of the final accounts). For example an amount for £38,000 posted to an account as £83,000 would cause the trial balance not to balance. A **compensating error** (i.e. an error which cancels itself out), would not be detected in a trial balance, nor would posting the correct amount to the wrong account. For the purpose of our demonstration, we will assume that all the errors listed have been found after the final accounts have been prepared.

In the case of a sale on credit where the invoice had been correctly recorded in sales and debtors, but the goods in question have not yet been deducted from the closing stock, the closing stock would be reduced by the cost of the stock which has been sold. This would increase the profit before tax and the retained earnings, i.e. closing stock down in value, retained earnings up by the same amount.

Mini-case: The late arrival of a purchase invoice

Redgrave Sprint Boats Ltd received an invoice for the supply of raw materials from Pin-cent plc for £15,000. The amount had been included in the closing stock figure for the period, but no entries had been made elsewhere.
Action The purchases figure would be increased by £15,000. This would cause a reduction in the net profit before tax, and a reduction in the retained earnings. The effect on the balance sheet would be:

Retained earnings reduced by £15,000
Creditors (in Current Liabilities) **increased by £15,000**

Mini-case: An item included in purchases and creditors but not included in the closing stock figure

This happened to Lin-daven-port Co. Ltd. An invoice for £7,200 for goods on credit had been posted correctly, but the whole amount had been excluded from the closing stock.
Action The closing stock value would increase by £7,200. This would cause the cost of sales to decrease and the net profit before tax (the bottom line) and the retained earnings to increase. The effect on the balance sheet would be:

Retained earnings increased by £7,200
Stock (in Current Assets) **increased by £7,200**

Alternative treatments of transactions
The impact of the prudence and materiality concepts
These two concepts do tend to reduce the profit figure, for example, providing for all possible losses such as bad debts, and charging (i.e. writing off) low value items in the profit and loss account, when the benefit from the items in question have not all been consumed or used up in the current financial period, for example, stationery, cleaning materials, and so on.

Capital and revenue expenditure
The division between the two categories is not always clear cut. To carry forward an expense into the future as a fixed asset, and to depreciate it over a period of years would spread the cost over its life. To charge it as an expense in the profit and loss account would have a one-off effect on the profit. One of the major areas where the distinction between capital and revenue expenditure is not so clear is repairs and renewals.

Changes in accounting policies
Companies do change their accounting policies and disclose the fact that this has been done in their annual report and accounts.

The changes will tend to affect the reported profit (or loss) and affect the value of the assets in the balance sheet. For example, changes in depreciation policy; changes in the way the stocks and work-in-progress values are arrived at.

What would happen if we doubled the depreciation charge?
The profit and the retained earnings would go down by the additional amount. The fixed asset net book value would go down by the same amount. Cash flow however, would not be affected at all because depreciation is non-cash.

Appropriations
The items which are dealt with in the profit and loss appropriation section will not have any effect on the profit before tax. The appropriation section does in fact show how the net profit before tax is shared up amongst the various stakeholders, for example, taxation, the shareholders and retained by the company.

Any alteration to the tax figure or dividends figure would be reflected by a corresponding change in the retained earnings figure which remains after any transfers to reserves.

Trends

When reviewed over a period of time, **trends** can be identified and extracted from the data, for example, growth in profits and sales by sector/sales area/product. The statistics produced could take inflation into account if/when appropriate.

The limitations of the profit and loss account and balance sheet

Accounting is *not an exact science*. The reported profit or loss and the picture portrayed by the balance sheet depend upon the *judgement* of those who prepare and audit them, and in particular the *application of the accounting concepts*. The recommendations of the various accounting standards are not mandatory unless their provisions have been incorporated into company law. The standard (SSAP2) *Disclosure of Accounting Policies* recognizes four fundamental accounting concepts: the accruals concept, the consistency concept, the going concern concept and the prudence concept.

The application of these and the other concepts is still open to many different interpretations. The balance sheet shows *the position at a particular moment in time*. The position could change significantly over a short space of time. In many cases the assets can never give a realistic valuation because they are shown at their *historic cost*, or *historic cost less depreciation*, or *net realizable value*.

There are quite a number of different ways of valuing stocks and work-in-progress. Some companies may have never re-valued all/some of their fixed assets, or re-valued them several years ago or quite recently. Some companies may have a lot or a little by way of 'off balance sheet financing', for example, renting or leasing equipment. Only items which can be measured in *monetary terms* are shown in a balance sheet, for example, items such as good industrial relations, managerial experience, and so on, cannot be shown.

Creative accounting and 'window dressing'

The application of the concepts and accounting policies mentioned above do provide scope for creativity. Other actions can also prove to be quite creative. For example, a special effort in the months leading up to the year end to collect outstanding debts and/or reduce stock levels would produce lower than normal debtors and closing stock figures. This would help to improve the various efficiency ratios which make use of those figures.

```
KEY WORDS
```

Statement of accounting policies	Realized profit
Capital reserve	Accounting standards (SSAPs)
Financial reporting standards (FRSs)	Write off
Goodwill	Capitalize
Intangible assets	Net realizable value
Re-valued	Secured lending
Trial balance	Compensating error
Trends	Creative accounting

Further reading

Atrill, P. & McLaney E. & Harvey D., Chapters 1–4 *Accounting for Business*, Butterworth-Heinemann, 2000.

Chadwick, L., Chapters 4, 5 & 8 *Essential Financial Accounting*, Financial Times Prentice Hall, 2001.

Dyson, J., Chapter 6 *Accounting for Non-Accounting Students*, Financial Times Prentice Hall, 2001.

Useful website

Pearson education website
www.pearsoneduc.com

Essay topics

1. (a) Distinguish between tangible and intangible assets. [7 marks]
   (b) Explain how the following assets should be treated in the profit and loss account, and balance sheet:
   - research and development expenditure [6 marks]
   - goodwill [6 marks]
   - patents [6 marks]

2. (a) Write up a specimen Accounting Policies section of a company's Annual Report and Accounts which covers: depreciation; stocks and work-in-progress; foreign currencies; eases. [10 marks]
   (b) Comment, with reasons, on whether or not you consider that the depreciation policy will enable the final accounts to give a true and fair view. [15 marks]

Chapter Five

Cash flow statements and the statutory published reports and accounts

'*Income £20 expenditure £19, happiness!*'
'*Income £20 expenditure £21, misery!*'
Adapted quotation from David Copperfield by Charles Dickens

'*A lack of concern with cash flow can be dangerous.*'
H.N. Woodward, Harvard Business Review, Jan/Feb 1976

'*Profitability and liquidity do not go hand in hand.*'
The author

The distinction between cash flow and profits

What is cash flow?

Cash flow is concerned with **liquidity**, i.e. the ability to pay the debts of the entity as the debts become due for payment. This is why it is important to produce cash flow forecasts (i.e. cash budgets) to ensure that funds are available when they are needed, and to identify problems and opportunities. Please note that the cash flow forecast which uses pre-determined figures is quite separate and different to the cash flow statement. The information from which the cash flow statement is constructed is historic, i.e. it looks backwards over the financial period. One very simple definition of cash flow published by *The Investors' Chronicle* is:

Cash flow = Net profit plus depreciation

(Depreciation is a non cash expense, the cash moves when the fixed asset in question is paid for.)

Why is it that profitability and liquidity do not go hand in hand?

When profits are generated they are represented eventually by an increase in cash. Cash also comes into the business from other sources, for example, ordinary share capital, debentures, loans, the sale of fixed assets and/or investments, and so on. The expenditure on new fixed assets, new investments, taxation and dividends, and so on, all represent cash out flows. If the company pays out more than it receives, this will have a negative impact on its cash and bank balances.

> ## Mini-case: Why has cash gor
> ## have gone
>
> Fremula Spicepersons, the managing direct
> problem. Fremula explained the problem. 'I d
> our profits for the year amounted to £7.2m b
> went up by £16m!' Fremula went on, 'This is
> someone in the accounts department made a

Financial Management

purchased, invest
outflows).

The answer to this question could be explained by looking at the company's cash flow statement. In addition to the profit of £7.2m, depreciation which is a non-cash flow was added back and funds were received from other sources, for example, share premium now received, an issue of debentures, and so on, which after deduction of **cash outflows** left an increase in the cash and bank balances of £16m. If you pay out less than you receive in cash your cash and bank balances will go up.

> ## Mini-case: It can happen to the best!
>
> Many years ago one very successful and profitable company almost went out of business because of cash flow problems. The company's name, Rolls Royce. Profitability and liquidity do not go hand in hand.

Cash flow statements (FRS 1)

The cash flow statement (may also be referred to as the funds flow statement or funds flow) which is included as part of the statutory published report and accounts of a company is the one which is prescribed by Financial Reporting Standard 1 (**FRS 1**). This provides a review of where all the cash from and how it was used during an accounting period. It is based on historic information and looks back, for example, at the year just ended, at the reasons for movements in cash. The format in which it is produced has six major headings, which are shown in Figure 10.

The information which is contained in the cash flow statement forms quite a logical but complex calculation. It is illustrating the point: that the increase or decrease in the cash and bank balances is caused by cash coming in from **operating activities** (after adjustment for movements in stocks, debtors, marketable securities and creditors, and so on) and non-operating activities plus new share capital and new loans/debentures, plus cash received from the sale of fixed assets and investments (**cash inflows**) and, after deducting dividends paid, tax paid, the cost of new fixed assets

...ents, and the repayment of any loans/debentures (cash

CASH FLOW STATEMENT (FRS 1)

- Net cash inflow/outflow from operating activities
- Returns on investments and the servicing of finance
- Taxation
- Investing activities
- Financing
- Increase (or decrease) in cash and cash equivalents

Figure 10 The six major headings in the cash flow statement (FRS 1)

We will now take a look at a more detailed FRS 1 cash flow statement for Greenhead Scientific Supplies PLC, in Figure 11.

GREENHEAD SCIENTIFIC INSTRUMENTS PLC

Cash Flow Statement for the year ended 31 December, 20X4.

	£million	£million
Net cash flow from operating activities:		
(Operating profit 142 plus Depreciation 72 less		
movements in stocks, debtors, marketable securities,		
creditors, and accruals 135)		79
Returns on investments, and the servicing of finance:		
Dividends paid *(last year's amount owing)*	(2)	
Interest paid	(41)	(43)
		36
Taxation:		
Tax paid *(last year's tax owing)*		(23)
		13
Investing activities:		
Purchase of tangible fixed assets *(56 + 104)*		(160)
Financing:		
Share premium	16	
Long-term loans and debentures	124	140
DECREASE IN CASH AND BANK BALANCES		(7)

Figure 11 The FRS 1 Cash Flow Statement

Points to note

The net cash flow from operating activities has had the depreciation of fixed assets added back and has also been adjusted for movements in current assets other than cash and bank balances, and creditors and accruals. Why make the adjustment? Answer – increases in stocks and debtors etc. represent more capital being tied up. Increases in creditors and accruals means more short-term financing coming from the suppliers of goods and services on credit (and vice-versa).

The **dividends** and **tax** paid were the amounts which were owing at the date of last year's balance sheet i.e. 20X3. Beware, the correct cash flow figure for dividends paid is last year's amount owing plus the interim dividend which has been paid for this year (if any).

Also note that in the UK the tax paid in cash during the year could have been different to the amount which was shown as owing in the 20X3 balance sheet. This is because the amount of tax payable has to be agreed with the Inland Revenue (i.e. tax authorities).

The interest paid was the actual amount which was paid during the year just ended, i.e. 20X4.

The depreciation charge and cost of new fixed assets was not given in the profit and loss account and balance sheet which we studied in Figures 9 and 11. In the statutory published report and accounts this information could be extracted from the notes to the accounts. Figure 12 shows you how we were able to track down this information for the cash flow statement.

The additional cash coming in from share premium and long term loans/debentures was simply the difference between the figures 20X3 and 20X4. One of the major purposes of the cash flow statement is to show how the increase or decrease in the cash and bank balances has come about.

Disclosure requirements of the statutory published reports and accounts of companies

The Companies Acts 1985/1989 direct minimum reporting requirements for the statutory published reports and accounts (**annual reports**) of companies. To go into great depth and detail is outside the scope of this text. We will however, take a look at some of the items which you are likely to come across when you look at some real company accounts.

The notes to the accounts

As mentioned earlier a vast amount of the information which companies are required to publish is shown in the **Notes to the accounts** section of the annual report together with corresponding figures for the previous year.

That the operating profit is after charging: depreciation; operating lease payments; audit fees (the amount of each would be shown).In the case of

Greenhead Scientific Supplies PLC the depreciation figure of £72m would be shown in this section.

- Non-operating exceptional items, for example, profits or losses on the sale of investments or fixed assets.
- Directors' remuneration, for example, salaries and share options.
- Staff costs, for example, wages, salaries, pensions, average number of people employed.
- Net interest receivable/payable.
- Taxation.
- Dividends, for example, on ordinary shares.
- Earnings per share.
- Tangible fixed assets – details of purchases/sales/transfers.

Figure 12 should give you a good idea of how the note relating to the Fixed Assets of Greenhead Scientific Supplies PLC could appear in the notes to accounts section of their annual report and accounts for 20X4.

Fixed Assets (£millions) 20X4	Cost	Depreciation to date	Net
Freehold land and buildings (1 Jan 20×4)	320	(20)	300
Additions	56		56
Depreciation of buildings		(6)	(6)
	376	26	350
Equipment, fixtures and fittings	400	(158)	242
Additions	104		104
Depreciation		(66)	(66)
	504	224	280

Freehold land held by the company amounting to £100 million has not been depreciated.
There were no sales of fixed assets during the period.

Figure 12 Notes to the accounts – details of fixed assets for Greenhead Scientific Supplies PLC

- Investments held as fixed assets, for example, shares at cost less amounts written off.
- Stocks, for example, raw materials and consumables, work-in-progress, and so on.
- Debtors: amounts falling due within one year.
- Creditors: amounts falling due within one year, for example, bank loans and overdrafts, trade creditors, other creditors, taxation, and dividends.

- Analysis of borrowings.
- **Share capital**, for example, authorized share capital, details of movements in share capital.
- Reserves – **movements in the reserves**, for example, profit and loss account, general reserve, share premium account, revaluation reserve etc.

KEY WORDS

Liquidity	Profitability
Cash inflows and outflows	FRS 1
Operating activities	Dividends
Tax	
Statutory published report & accounts	Annual Report
Notes to the accounts	Movements in reserves
Share capital	Analysis of borrowings

Further reading

Chadwick, L., Chapter 6 *Essential Financial Accounting for Managers*, Financial Times Prentice Hall, 2001.

Davies, D., Chapter 5 *The Art of Managing Finance*, McGraw-Hill, 1997.

Dyson, J., Chapter 8 *Accounting for Non-Accounting Students*, Financial Times Prentice Hall, 2001.

Essay topics

1. (a) Explain what is meant by 'cash flow' [10 marks]
   (b) Discuss what can cause an increase in a company's cash and bank balances. [15 marks]

2. (a) Distinguish between profitability and liquidity. [10 marks]
   (b) Discuss why profitability and liquidity may not go hand in hand. [15 marks]

Chapter Six

The interpretation and analysis of the final accounts

'It's not the ratios themselves that are important, but the questions which they provoke.' Colin Drury in his MBA Dissertation, University of Bradford Management Centre, 1976.

'To make any sense of ratios, you need several years' figures and to make valid comparisons you need to obtain appropriate industry figures to use as a benchmark.' Leslie Chadwick

An introduction to financial performance analysis

The management of a company/organization are forever trying to assess their financial performance to assist them with their decision-making, and to ensure that the scarce resources are being used efficiently. In so doing, they like to review their financial performance over a period of several years, and compare their financial performance with that of similar companies. This should enable them to identify emerging trends, strengths and weaknesses. To further assist their quest to make useful and valid comparisons, they also make use of **industry averages** (industry figures), and use these as a **benchmark** against which to measure and compare their own financial performance. The principal tool which is used to assess financial performance is ratio analysis. There are however, other ways of assessing performance, for example, VFM (value for money auditing) which is a very useful way of assessing services such as education, libraries and the health service. This could involve expressing costs as the cost per student, cost per patient, and so on, so that comparisons can be made, reported on, and appropriate action taken. Another way which is growing in popularity is the balanced scorecard approach; this uses financial and other measures, such as ratios, customers and internal business processes.

Ratio analysis and the interpretation of financial statements

The ratios used to assess financial performance need to be used in conjunction with other data/information. They enable the management to focus their time and attention on areas which need to be improved or investigated further and provoke numerous questions. The areas of ratio analysis which we will look at are as follows: **profitability, liquidity, efficiency, capital structure, employees, investment.**

In order to illustrate the calculations of the ratios we will, where possible, use the information which is contained in the profit and loss account, and the balance sheet of Greenhead Scientific Supplies PLC as shown in Figures 6 and 9 which we looked at earlier on in this text.

Profitability

According to some of the American writers the real name of the business game is **ROI** (return on investment). In the UK we tend to talk about **ROCE** or ROC (return on capital employed or return on capital), which means the same thing. Business is all about putting in money (i.e. investing in the business), and getting a satisfactory return. Such a return should reward investors for the amount which they have invested and also compensate them for the risk which they have undertaken.

Another name for this ratio is the return on net assets. The net assets i.e. total assets less current liabilities, for example, for 20X4 £848million and described as 'The Employment of Capital' is the same figure as the Capital Employed figure in Figure 9.

Gross profit to sales (also called the 'mark-up' or 'gross margin')

This ratio indicates the average mark-up which is being earned on the products or services provided by the company/organization to its customers. Movements in this ratio will also account for some of the movements in the ratios which use the net profit figure. Insurance companies find this ratio very useful when it comes to estimating the amount of stock which has been lost in a fire or flood.

The gross profit/sales ratio for Greenhead Scientific Supplies would be:

(£millions)	
20X4	**20X3**
$\dfrac{868}{3,218} \times 100 = 26.97\%$	$\dfrac{503}{1,867} \times 100 = 26.94\%$

Is this a good or bad performance? Answer: a slight improvement from last year, possibly caused by charging slightly higher prices and/or more efficient purchasing and/or reducing waste/scrap. If the industry average is 18.67%, then this is a very good performance. If the industry average is 29.45%, it would be a poor performance. However, this could be due to under-pricing certain products in order to gain a foothold in the market, or giving generous trade discounts on large orders.

Net profit to sales (net margin)
This may be calculated:

(NPBT)	$\dfrac{\text{Net profit before tax}}{\text{Sales}}$	$\times$	100

20×4	20×3
$\dfrac{101}{3,218} \times 100 = 3.14\%$	$\dfrac{49}{1,867} \times 100 = 2.62\%$

This shows how much profit is being generated per £100 of sales revenue. An increase in this figure could be the result of better management of the overhead expenses, for example, heating and lighting, cleaning, administration, and so on, i.e. anything which improves the 'bottom line'.

Return on capital employed (ROCE)
When it comes to assessing the return on capital employed there are a number of ways in which it may be computed, for example, using the profit before tax, the profit after tax, and so on. One of the ways is to use the **net profit before interest and tax (NPBIT)**. This return on investment measure provides an indication of the productivity of the capital employed irrespective of the source from which it came. To calculate it we have to add back the interest on loans/debentures to the net profit before tax.

(£millions)	20X4	20X3
Net profit before tax	101	49
Add back interest paid	41	20
NPBIT =	142	69

(In this example the NPBIT was the same as the operating profit. This is not always the case as there may be other income that affects the calculation.)

$$\frac{142}{848} \times 100 = 16.75\% \qquad \frac{69}{656} \times 100 = 10.52\%$$

The improvement could be due to what has already been mentioned in relation to the 'bottom line', the effects of gearing (see *Capital Structure*), more efficient use being made of the fixed assets, for example, making use of idle capacity, and/or 'off-balance-sheet financing', i.e. renting or leasing fixed assets.

Return on ordinary shareholders' funds
This is calculated:

$$\frac{\text{Net profit after tax (NPAT)}}{\text{Ordinary share capital} + \text{reserves}} \times 100$$

This ratio is also called the return on equity, (remember, that the ordinary share capital plus reserves may be described as **equity**). Also note that if there were any preference shares, then the preference share dividends for the year would be deducted from the net profit after tax. The amount which is left belongs to the ordinary shareholders. However, remember that the rewards which ordinary shareholders receive are two-fold: dividends, and capital gains (or capital losses). This ratio does provide them with a benchmark against which to measure and compare their investment. For example, to compare with high interest bank or building society interest rates. Their returns for 20X4 and 20X3 are:

20X4	20X3
$\frac{54}{276} \times 100 = 19.57\%$	$\frac{26}{208} \times 100 = 12.5\%$

There has been a significant improvement between the two years. This could have been caused by all of the factors which affect the net profit after tax including the gearing. If higher interest bank accounts are currently paying around 8% gross this does help to compensate for the additional risk which investing in ordinary shares entails. This ratio could also be considered under the heading of *investment ratios* as it provides existing and would-be investors with a benchmark (yard-stick) against which to compare investment performance.

Liquidity

However profitable a company may be, if it cannot pay its debts as the debts become due for payment it could go out of business, for example, by being wound up or taken over. Liquidity ratios provide an indication of solvency and the ability of the company to pay its way. You should note that we do not tend to express these ratios as a percentage.

Current assets to current liabilities

	20X4		20X3	
Current assets	430	= 2.028	266	= 1.75
Current liabilities	212		152	

The ratio has improved. For every £1 owing to the current liabilities the company has approximately £2.03p of cover compared to £1.75p of cover for 20X3.

The acid test (or quick) ratio

This ratio divides the liquid assets, i.e. current assets less the stock/inventories figure, by the current liabilities. The liquid assets are: *20X4 430 less 150 = 280* and *20X3 266 less 65 = 201*. The calculation of this ratio for the two years will be:

$$\frac{280}{212} = 1.32 \qquad \frac{201}{152} = 1.32$$

For each of the years in question, for every £1 owing to current liabilities there is £1.32p cover. As a general rule, it is considered that this ratio should be around one to one (1: 1). In practice, many companies do tend to work on a ratio which is slightly less than 1:1, for example, for certain industries the industry average could be around 0.86:1. Higher than average ratios could be a sign of poor **working capital management.** For example poor control of stocks, debtors, cash, and may be, paying creditors too quickly.

Efficiency

The efficiency ratios which we will review cover the use of certain fixed and current assets, and the short-term finance provided by the creditors.

Average collection period

This tells us how long it is taking the company to collect the amounts owing from credit customers (i.e. their debtors). The system employed by companies/other organizations to ensure that the amounts owing are collected quickly and efficiently, and the granting of credit to customers, is called the **credit control** system. Improvements to the system could include cutting down the time period (the lead time) between delivering or providing the goods and services on credit and sending out the invoice; or simply ringing slow payers up to find out why they have not paid, for example, it could be the company's own fault, the customer could be just waiting for a credit note, which has not yet been sent out. This can be calculated in a number of ways, one of which is as follows:

Average debtors divided by sales multiplied by 365. For 20X4 the average debtors figure would be the 20X4 debtors £236 plus the 20X3 debtors £142 divided by 2 giving £189.

20X4

$$\frac{\text{Average debtors £189}}{\text{Sales 3,218}} \times 365 = 21.44 \text{ days}$$

If other companies are taking on average around 45 days, then it would be an excellent performance. However, this could have come about by allowing over generous cash discounts for prompt payment. A small percentage discount for early settlement of an account can have a very high APR (annual percentage rate of interest). In cases where there is insufficient data to calculate the average debtors figure, all we can do is use the debtors figure for the current year.

Credit period provided by the creditors (credit period taken)

Here, we use the average creditors divided by the purchases (if available) multiplied by 365 to convert it into days. The purchases for Greenhead Scientific Supplies PLC for 20X4 amounted to £2,345m. The average creditors and accrued expenses amount to £145m. This gives:

Thus, on average, the company is paying its suppliers of goods and serv-

20X4

$$\frac{\text{Average creditors £145}}{\text{Purchases £2,345}} \times 365 = 22.57 \text{ days}$$

ices on credit within 23 days. This may be around the standard for this industry. If however the average within the industry is say 40 days, it is paying up far too quickly, unless it is doing so in order to take advantage of generous early settlement discounts.

The rate of stock turnover and the stock holding period

Stocks and inventories represent capital tied up in goods. The more that is held, and the longer it is held, the more costly it becomes to the business. The holding of stocks has to be financed and also involves expensive **holding costs**, for example, lighting, heating and cleaning of the warehouse, insurance, administrative costs, and so on.

The rate of stock turnover = Sales divided by the average stock (the average stock is the opening stock £65 for 20X3 + £150 for 20X4 divided by 2 = £107.5).

The rate of turnover is: $\dfrac{\text{Sales } 3{,}218}{\text{Ave. stock } 107.5} = 29.93 \text{ times}$

The stock holding period can be calculated as follows:

$\dfrac{365 \text{ days}}{\text{Rate of turnover}} \quad \dfrac{365}{29.93} = 12.20 \text{ days}$

This is quite a rapid rate of turnover: approximately 12 days, which means less capital tied up for long periods and a reduced risk of losses caused by deterioration and/or obsolescence. To improve the stock (inventory) control/ performance in this case may be difficult, but it may still be possible to reduce the holding time further by: disposing of surplus and obsolete stocks (if any); making frequent reviews of maximum, minimum and re-order levels; and introducing a **JIT** (just in time) system, a system in which the goods arrive from suppliers and within a short space of time are put into the production process, for example, within 24–48 hours for certain companies producing motor components.

Sales to fixed assets

This is a productivity measure which says that for every pound invested in fixed assets the company will generate x pounds worth of sales. It can use all of the fixed assets or just the manufacturing fixed assets. The company's performance for this measure is:

20X4	20X3
$\dfrac{\text{Sales } 3{,}218}{\text{Fixed assets } 630} = \text{£5.11}$	$\dfrac{1{,}867}{542} = \text{£3.44}$

In 20X4 every pound invested in fixed assets generates £5.11 sales, an improvement on 20X3. The fixed asset utilization has improved. Here also, the picture could be affected by 'off-balance-sheet financing' and the re-valuation of fixed assets. For example, an increase in the value of fixed assets next year is likely to make the utilization of fixed assets look worse.

Capital structure and gearing

Gearing

Gearing (called leverage in the USA) is sometimes referred to as **debt v equity**: debt being long-term loans, debentures, and preference shares (but note that preference shares are in certain circumstances treated as being part of the equity!) and equity being ordinary share capital plus reserves. Those companies which are highly geared, i.e. that have a high proportion of debt compared to equity, are also higher risk. If there are poor trading conditions, for example, during a recession, even though a company may be making losses it still has to pay interest on loans and debentures. Thus, highly geared companies are in greater danger of going out of business.

There are lots of gearing calculations, all of which look at the relationship between debt and equity. One such calculation is:

$$\frac{\text{Debt, i.e. long-term loans and debentures}}{\text{Debt plus equity}} \times 100$$

What is high and low will depend upon the averages for the industry in which the company operates. The gearing ratio for each year will be:

20X4	20X3
$\dfrac{572}{848} \times 100 = 67.45\%$	$\dfrac{448}{656} \times 100 = 68.29\%$

If the industry average is 60% then 67% is on the high side. To get more long-term financing for the future may mean that it will have to come from retained earnings or more ordinary share capital.

Interest cover

This provides an indication of how many times the net profit before interest and tax (NPBIT) is able to cover the interest payments. For the two years, this works out as follows:

20X4	20X3
$\dfrac{\text{NPBIT } 142}{\text{Interest } 41} = 3.46$	$\dfrac{69}{20} = 3.45$

The company has been able to maintain its interest cover. If the industry average is 3.20 this is good. However, with the high level of gearing, if the profits fall the company could experience problems.

Employee ratios

There are a number of employee ratios many of which measure the productivity of labour in financial terms, for example, sales per employee; net profit per employee, and so on.

Investment

Two of the most well-known and well-used investment ratios are the **EPS** (**earnings per share**) and the **PE ratio** (**price/earnings ratio**). For the purpose of our calculations we will assume that Greenhead Scientific Supplies PLC's market price per share was £3.60 for 20X4 and £3.20 for 20X3.

Earnings per share (EPS)

The net profit after tax (NPAT) less any preference dividend is divided by the number of ordinary shares. **Why?** The profit figure which remains after deducting tax and any preference dividends all belongs to the ordinary shareholders. The EPS for the last two years is as follows:

20X4	20X3
$\dfrac{\text{NPAT } 54}{120^*} = £0.45\text{p per share}$	$\dfrac{26}{120^*} = £0.216\text{p per share}$

* This is the number of issued ordinary shares.

The dramatic increase in the net profit after tax divided by the same number of shares has lead to a very significant increase in the EPS. The company could now well be reaping the benefits of the high gearing.

Price/earnings ratio (PE ratio)

To compute this ratio we divide the market price per share by the earnings per share. Remember that the share price is affected by many factors, for example, sales growth, market share, profits, dividends and in particular market expectations. The **PE ratios** for the two years are:

	20X4	20X3
$\dfrac{\text{Market pice per share}}{\text{Earnings per share}}$	$\dfrac{3.60}{.45} = 8$	$\dfrac{3.20}{.216} = 14.81$

The higher PE for 20X3 could in the main be caused by high market expectations.

Mini-case: Buying dogs!

A 'dog type company' may be described as a company which is low on growth in terms of sales and low on cash. Such companies tend to have low price to earnings ratios. This is because of their poor financial performance and market perceptions and expectations.

Once upon a time, a UK entrepreneur's strategy was to buy companies with low PE ratios, i.e. the market did not expect much of them. Having taken them over, together with his management team he would turn them around over a period of several years, for example, 4 years and then sell them. As time went by, as soon as he acquired the 'dog type company' the share price went up because the market expected better things to come and a brighter future for the company. He became a millionaire. His name, Sir John Templeton.

Over-trading

This occurs when a business tries to trade at a level of activity greater than it is financially equipped for. Some of the possible signs of **over-trading** are: the overdraft is at the limit; using working capital to finance long-term assets; cash flow problems which may result in very efficient inventory control and stock control systems. Such businesses may be very keen on growth. However, growth for growth's sake is not always a good strategy. The business needs to make profits and manage its cash flow.

Information which is needed in addition to the financial information

The financial performance analysis is just one component part of the jigsaw. It needs to be looked at in conjunction with other data/statistics.

Other information which may prove to be very useful includes:

- **SWOT analysis** (strengths, weaknesses, opportunities, threats) for the company/organization concerned and their competitors.
- Information gained from **monitoring the environment** in which the entity operates, for example, political, technological, and so on.
- Statistical data from Government Departments, Chambers of Trade, research firms, professional journals, www sources, and so on.
- A review of the company's own products/services/customer service levels etc. and those of competitors. For example a review of product life cycles. This could indicate whether or not the product or service has now reached the market saturation stage or the decline stage.
- Stock market information, for example, information about the performance of the Company's own shares and those of other companies/competitors within the sector.
- Information about the future. For example, the expected rate of inflation, what will happen to interest rates, and the level of output/activity. For internal purposes, budgets, policies and objectives.

How to produce a financial performance analysis

Figure 13, which is illustrated below, provides you with a specimen layout for carrying out a financial analysis of a company.

Ratio	This* Year 20X5	Last Year 20X4	Variance +or−	Reasons for variance/ comments
Turnover	£531m	£542m		
Earnings per share	24.4p	11.75p		
Dividend cover	3.0 times	1.4 times		

There would be sections for Liquidity, Profitability, Cover etc. (followed by conclusions – remember that Liquidity and Profitability do not go hand in hand).
*Could be Firm A compared with Firm B, useful also to compare industry statistics

Figure 13 Interpretation of accounts

You should note that by completing the narrative (i.e. the reasons for the variance/comments section), which also involves looking for possible inter-relationships between the ratios, that you will in fact be identifying strengths and weaknesses. Having completed the analysis using this working notes system you should be in a very good position to write up the conclusions and recommendations section of the financial analysis.

The limitations of financial performance analysis

Much fairer financial performance comparisons can be carried out within the same company/group of companies, i.e. **internal comparisons**. **External comparisons**, i.e. comparing financial performance with other companies, can never be as fair or accurate.

The principal financial statements which are used, i.e. the profit and loss accounts, and balance sheets are historical documents and, to a large extent, depend upon the way in which the concepts and the accounting policies have been applied. For example: the depreciation policy, the concepts of materiality, prudence, entity etc. You will recall, that the balance sheet is prepared as at a certain date and that the figures which it contains can be can be affected by: creative accounting, 'off-balance-sheet financing' and the re-valuation of fixed assets.

The way in which the ratios are calculated also causes numerous questions. For example:

- Which profit figure should we use?
- Which capital employed figure should we include?
- Which share price should we adopt?
- Is the average stock or debtors or creditors representative of the position which existed throughout the year?

Who to compare with

Comparisons are more valid if they are made with the sector average rather than the industry average. When selecting companies with which to compare, you need to choose a company/s of a similar size in the same sector with: a similar product portfolio; the same year end; and a similar number of employees etc.

KEY WORDS

Industry averages	Benchmark
Profitability	Liquidity
Efficiency	Capital structure
Employee ratios	Investment ratios
ROI	ROCE
NPBIT	'Off-balance-sheet financing'
Equity	Credit control
Working capital management	Holding costs
JIT (just-in-time)	Gearing
Debt v equity	EPS (earnings per share)
PE ratio (price/earnings)	Over-trading
SWOT analysis	Monitoring the environment
Internal and external comparisons	

Further reading

Chadwick, L., Chapter 7 *Essential Financial Accounting for Managers*, Financial Times Prentice Hall, 2001.

Davies, D., Chapter 4 *The Art of Managing Finance*, McGraw-Hill, 1997.

Dodge, R., Chapter 13, *Foundations of Business Accounting*, Business Press Thomson Learning, 2000.

Pizzey, A., Chapter 6 *Finance and Accounting for Non-Specialist Students*, Financial Times Prentice Hall, 1998.

Wood, F. and Sangster, A., Part 7 *Business Accounting 1*, Financial Times Prentice Hall, 1999.

Useful website

Ratio analysis

www.learn.co.uk/default.asp

Essay topics and projects

1. Explain and illustrate why profitability and liquidity do not always go 'hand in hand'. [25 marks]

2. Discuss, giving your reasons, which profitability ratios you consider will be of great interest to:
   (a) the management of the company [8 marks]
   (b) the shareholders of the company [8 marks]
   (c) prospective investors. [8 marks]

Case Study

Financial performance in premier league football

Football in the UK has become 'big business'. Key clubs in the industry, because of their need for significant injections of finance, have become public companies and are now quoted on the London Stock Exchange. There does appear to be a strong link between financial success and success on the football field. Premiership football clubs now receive vast sums of money from gate receipts, television rights, sponsorship, advertising, merchandising, corporate entertaining and other activities.

The current climate is now one of rising signing on fees, for example Aimbry United have recently had their offer of a £16 million signing on fee turned down for Vasco Chad van Sweeper, and Mirvale City recently gave a £12 million signing on fee for Figaro Les Henry, an international goal keeper. Players in the top flight are also demanding very high salaries.

As a result, all football clubs of any significant size have been considering strategies to assure them of a continuous and reliable supply of short-term and long-term financing. In addition, they have become much more marketing oriented and developed their brand names and merchandising activities.

You have been provided with the following information for three UK premier league football clubs: Mirvale City; Aimbry United and Lockwood Rangers.

Profit and Loss Account and Balance Sheet Data for 20×7/8:

Amounts in £000

20X7/8	*City*	*United*	*Rangers*
Turnover	37,741	53,316	8,990
Cost of sales	3,667	17,396	6,170
Capital employed	40,711	54,462	1,367
Shareholders funds	37,436	40.762	1,310
Loans	3,275	13,700	57
Tangible fixed assets	35,093	61,295	633
Intangible fixed assets	10,215	0	19
Current assets	17,668	32,397	5,027
Current liabilities	17,705	22,060	4,312
Stock	289	2,072	720
Average trade debtors	2,560	6,560	3,612
Average stock	2,385	2,038	720
Operating profit (loss)	12,374	14,167	162
Profit (loss) before interest and tax	12,309	15,925	172

Turnover Growth

Five Year Financial Summary

	20X7/8	20X6/7	20X5/6	20X4/5	20X3/4
City	37,341	25,083	22,326	25,265	19,308
United	53,316	60,622	43,815	15,177	20,145
Rangers	8,990	5,196	5,333	770	550

Required:

1. From the information provided, compare the financial performance of the three football clubs for 20X7/8, and comment on their growth in turnover.
2. Discuss the reasons/problems associated with raising additional funds via: a new issue of ordinary shares; a 'rights issue'; convertible debentures.
3. What other ways of increasing revenue are being used or could be investigated?
4. Which post-balance sheet events can significantly affect the picture which has been portrayed by the annual report and accounts?
5. Is premiership football a sport or a business?

Chapter Seven
Cost and management accounting

Over one hundred years ago, in 1889 when Queen Victoria was on the throne of England, George Pepler Norton had his book entitled *Textile Manufacturer's Book-Keeping* published. In it he described innovations in cost accounting as being 'for the most part useless and often mischievous'.

An introduction to cost and management accounting

The role of the cost and management accountant has been described as being that of an **information manager**. Management accounting does make use of historic costs, but is much more concerned with pre-determined costs i.e. estimated costs which relate to the future. It aims at providing information which will help management with their decision-making, and enable them to control and monitor business operations. For example, **target setting** for sales, spending, production, via budgets. Such targets can act as motivators (or de-motivators if they are impossible to achieve). Another essential element, is **reporting**, for example, Figure 14 illustrates one of the ways in which this operates.

Figure 14 cost and management reporting system

The reporting system in Figure 14 would help to control costs and revenues (for example, sales) by reporting performance at frequent intervals. Those performances which are well off-course will be highlighted so as to direct management into considering the most appropriate form of corrective action. It provides management with an early warning of things which are not going according to plan, and requires them to focus on matters which really need their attention, i.e. it motivates them into action. Solving problems earlier can bring about huge cost savings and avoid possible losses.

However, you should note that the pre-determined targets/figures are simply estimates and may be very poor estimates, and therefore not really suitable for measuring and comparing performance. **GIGO** (i.e. **garbage in, garbage out**): the benefits from such a system can be no better than the reliability of the original data. In setting targets, assumptions have to be

65

made about the future, for example, the rate of inflation, the level of output/activity, the economic climate, taxation levels, pay settlements, and so on. If there is a significant change in the assumptions, the targets should be reviewed and revised.

What is cost?

The first answer is, which cost? There are several different types of cost. Costs can be: historic; pre-determined; replacement costs; standard costs; and opportunity costs, that is the cost of the lost opportunity, for example, investing in a project compared with investing in a high interest account (the interest which would have been received being the lost opportunity).

Cost classification

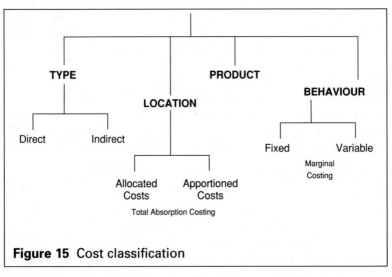

Figure 15 Cost classification

Costs may be classified in a number of ways. Some of the ways are as illustrated in Figure 15 above. A brief description of each classification is as follows:

Direct cost

These form part of the product or service or can be traced to a specific product or service. For example, raw materials and components which form part of a product; advertising for a specific product or service.

Indirect costs

They do not form part of the product or service. For example, cleaners wages or salaries, cleaning materials, rent of buildings, insurance of buildings, maintenance labour, material costs and so on. You should note that another widely used description of indirect costs is **overhead costs** or the **overheads**.

Location

Costs can be shared up between various locations, for example, departments, groups of machines, sub-groups, functions such as administration an so on. All of these locations can be described as **cost centres** i.e. a centre to which costs are charged and accumulated, or if they are revenue earning they can then be described as a **profit centre**. (All of this will become much clearer to you when we look at total absorption costing in the next chapter.)

Product or service

Here costs are assigned to each individual product or service.

Behaviour

Fixed costs – those costs which remain unchanged irrespective of the level of output within a relevant range. Lots of the fixed costs tend to vary more with time than output, for example, rent of buildings, insurance of buildings, administrative salaries, machinery which is on a fixed rental charge, and so on.

Variable costs – those costs which vary directly with the level of output/activity within a relevant range. For example, materials and components which form part of the product, the rent of machinery paid for at so much per unit which is produced and so on.

There are also combinations of the two, semi-variable and semi-fixed. For example, someone who receives a fixed salary plus a bonus based on output or sales.

The elements of cost

> The elements of cost are made up of the 'prime' (or direct) cost, plus the overheads, as follows:
>
> **Prime** (or direct **cost**):
> Direct materials
>   plus
> Direct labour
>   plus
> Direct expenses
>   plus
> The overheads (i.e. the indirect materials, indirect labour and indirect expenses)
>
> **Figure 16** The elements of cost

Mini-case: How do you cost something?

On a visit to the University of Linz in Austria, I was asked to give a short lecture to their older more mature degree students, about how to cost a feasibility study. I produced a slide which read, 'How do you cost a feasibility study?' This was quickly followed by another slide which read, 'ANSWER. In exactly the same was as you try to cost anything else!'

The cost of any product or service is made up of the **elements of cost**. However, this is not always such an easy and straightforward task. The cost of the direct materials and direct labour are both affected by **quantity and price**.

With direct materials we can work out the quantity of the materials which are needed to produce the product, for example, for motor components there will be a parts list for each product which details all of the parts which are needed; for the production of chemicals and confectionery there will be a recipe or standard mix of the ingredients. The pricing side of materials does present complications. A choice of the pricing method to be used has to be made, for example, from FIFO (first in, first out), LIFO (last in, first out), AVECO (average cost), and there are others.

In the case of direct labour, the quantity to be used to produce the product or service can be worked out using historic data, for example, the payroll analysis, and information about the future. The pricing side of labour is not without its problems. Some employees doing the same job may be on different rates of pay and then there is the question of how to account for shift work payments, overtime and incentive bonus payments. Some of the direct expenses will tend to be bought out services, and so on, and will have to be estimated or obtained via tenders or quotations, for example, drawings from a graphic designer; distribution services. The biggest problem however is how much should we include in the cost of the product or service to cover the overheads? We will attempt to answer this question in the next chapter by looking at two approaches to this problem, total absorption costing and marginal costing.

Cost units

One of the quests in management accounting is for a 'benchmark' or 'yardstick', i.e. an objective measure which can be used for analysis and comparative purposes. One of the ways in which costs can be compared is by using cost units, for example, the cost per hour, the cost per patient, cost per student, and so on. Several examples of cost units which are appropriate for certain types of business/organization are given in the table below.

Costs may be described as so much per unit and examples of cost units are as follows:

Business	Cost Unit
Brewing	Barrel
Brick-making	1,000 Bricks
Coal mining	Ton/tonne
Electricity	KWh (Kilowatt/Hours)
Engineering	Contract, job
Gas	Therm
Petroleum	Barrel, tonne, litre
Steel	Tonne/ton/sheet
Timber	100ft
Hotel and Catering	Room/cover
Professional Service (accountants, architects, lawyers, surveyors)	Chargeable hour
Education	(a) Enrolled student
	(b) Successful student
	(c) School Meal
Healthcare (hospitals)	(a) Bed occupied
	(b) Out-patient
Credit control	Account maintained
Materials storage/handling	Requisition
Personnel administration	Employee

Selling	(a) £ of turnover
	(b) Call made
	(c) Order taken
Telephone Service	Call made

Source: Management Accounting Official Terminology of The Chartered Institute of Management Accountants. (CIMA)

Product pricing

Mini-case: Is the price right?

Fly on a wall comment. 'We worked out all of our costs, including something to cover our overheads. We then added on a 60% mark-up to fix our selling price. This was a disaster, our competitors were beating us on price by between 15% and 20%!'

This scenario makes a very important point. The point being that whatever pricing system or pricing strategy you adopt, you cannot ignore the prices that are being charged by your **competitors**.

Mini-Case: An insurance claim

A true story. It's never our fault. The cost of repairing the damage to our vehicles caused by other road users is worked out as follows:
Materials used priced at the average cost, plus the labour hours at the labour rate, and then adding on 50% of the total of the materials and labour costs to cover the overheads. We then claim this amount from the insurance company involved!

Although this was historic costing, i.e. costing after the event, the treatment of the overheads was not very scientific, was it?

Cost-plus pricing
The direct cost (prime cost) of materials, labour and expenses is computed, plus overheads and then a mark-up (margin) is added to give the selling price or the price which will be used in a quotation.

Marginal cost pricing
The price is fixed to cover the marginal cost, i.e. the variable cost and to make a contribution towards the recovery of the fixed overheads.

Mini-case: A sprat to catch a mackerel!

The pricing strategy used for certain key customers was often referred to as 'a sprat to catch a mackerel' by a company engaged in the production of motor components. In order to gain a foothold in the market, it targeted certain key companies with exceptional value for money deals. To do this it priced certain of its products at their variable cost plus a small margin. This strategy proved to be quite successful.

You should also note that price is just one part of the marketing mix when assessing the offerings of competitors.

KEY WORDS

Information manager	Target setting
Reporting	GIGO (garbage in, garbage out)
Direct and indirect costs	Overhead cost (overheads)
Cost centre	Profit centre
Fixed cost	Variable cost
Prime cost	Elements of cost
Quantity and price	Competitors
Cost-plus pricing	Marginal cost pricing

Further reading

Atrill, P. & McLaney E., Chapter 1 *Management Accounting for Non-Specialists*, Financial Times Prentice Hall, 2001.

Chadwick, L., Chapter 1 *Essential Management Accounting*, Financial Times Prentice Hall, 2001.

Drury, C., Chapters 1 & 2 *Costing: an Introduction*, International Thomson Business Press, 1998.

Hussey, J. & Hussey R., Chapter 1 *Cost and Management Accounting*, Macmillan Business Masters, 1998.

Useful websites

Management and Cost Accounting – useful for this chapter, and all remaining chapters in this text.
www.drury-online.com
Cost management strategies
www.kellogg.nwu.edu/exec_edu/course/costmngt/cost_OOO.htm
An optimal pricing scheme
www.press.umich.edu/jep/works/WangOptPri.html

Essay topics

1. Explain the role of the management accountant and the management accounting function, in both public and private sector organizations.

[25 marks]

2. (a) How should we arrive at the cost of a product or service?

[10 marks]

(b) Discuss the problems which are associated with the costing of products or services.

[15 marks]

Data response question

1. Study the information on page 73 and answer **all** parts of the following question.

(a) Explain the term 'variable costs' (line 11). [3 marks]

(b) Sean plans to increase the number of holidays sold each week from 80 to 120 by lowering his price. Calculate the effects this will have on the company's weekly profits if his estimates prove correct. [8 marks]

(c) Sean's accountant has warned that his forecasts are optimistic and that a cut in prices may not increase Sperrin Activity Holidays' profits. Examine two reasons why this might be the case. [8 marks]

(b) Sean says 'small businesses should worry more about cash flow than profits when expanding'. To what extent do you agree with this statement? [11 marks]

Sperrin Activity Holidays Ltd

Sean Morris left teaching several years ago to establish Sperrin Activity Holidays Ltd in a rural part of Northern Ireland. The company offers horse riding, walking, climbing and water sports holidays. Customers enjoy accommodation and first-class catering as well as excellent facilities and unspoilt countryside.

The UK market for activity holidays is fiercely price competitive and Sean Morris recognises that the sales of holidays are very dependent upon the prices he charges.

Weekly Sales of Holidays	Average Selling Price £	Total Variable Costs £
40	800	15 000
60	750	22 000
80	700	30 000
100	650	38 000
Fixed costs = £10 000 each week		

Equally, Sean is aware that his costs and profits depend upon the number of customers his business attracts each month. Sperrin Holidays currently sells an average of 80 holidays each week. Sean is seeking to expand his business. He estimates that if he lowers his price to £600 per holiday he will initially achieve 120 sales each week although total variable costs will rise to £43 000. With increased marketing he anticipates that sales will rise further in the future.

Sean's accountant thinks he is too optimistic and is concerned that a decision to reduce prices might not result in the company's profits rising, certainly in the short-run. Sean is not worried, arguing that 'small businesses should worry more about cash flow than profits when expanding'.

AQA Unit 1, Q2, AS Level January 2001

Chapter Eight

Costing methods – total absorption costing and marginal costing

'Total absorption costing is simply an attempt to ensure that all costs are covered.

'Marginal costing is the system which is recommended for decision making purposes, but has to be used with a great deal of care.'

The author

Total absorption costing

Total absorption costing, which can also be described as absorption costing or simply total costing includes certain overheads (indirect costs) in the cost of the product or service, for example, the production overheads.

Figure 17 explains how total absorption costing works.

Stages

1–3   Overheads estimated, and then allocated or apportioned to cost centres, for example, production and service departments, administration, and so on

4   Service department costs are shared out between users

5–6   Absorption (recovery) rates are calculated and the overheads charged to products, jobs or services

7   Should we include any administration, selling or distribution overheads in the costs of the products, jobs or services?

Figure 17 The absorption of overheads

A review of Figure 17, together with the following step-by-step notes, should help you to picture and understand just how this method works.

Stage 1. The overheads have to be estimated before the start of the forthcoming period. This will involve looking at past performance/records updated to take account of all future known/expected happenings/events.

Stage 2. Those overheads which can be **identified and traced** to a department/location (termed as the 'cost centre') are **allocated** to the cost centres concerned, for example, the cost of a cleaner whose hours can be traced to a specific location/locations.

Stage 3. Overheads which cannot be identified and traced to cost centres such as rent of premises, canteen and welfare costs, are **apportioned** to cost centres using some **equitable basis**, for example, shared in proportion to: the floor area, or cubic capacity, or the number of employees.

Stage 4. Service department costs are then apportioned to user departments, for example, the stores cost could be shared according to the number of stores requisitions/issue notes, others may be shared up on the basis of technical estimates.

Stage 5. Overhead **absorption rates** (also called **recovery rates**) are calculated for each production department cost centre, for example, using the estimated number of **machine hours** or **direct labour hours**.

Stage 6. Overheads are absorbed, i.e. charged to the products at so much per machine hour or direct labour hour. Products therefore, in effect, 'clock up' and accumulate a share of the overheads as they spend time in each cost centre. Hence the description, 'overhead accumulation'.

Stage 7. Decisions then have to be made on whether or not to include administration costs and/or selling and distribution costs in the cost of the product or service, and if so, on what basis.

You should note that where selling and/or distribution costs are incurred for a specific product or service, they can be treated as a direct cost of the product or service concerned and are not overheads, i.e. indirect costs.

Total absorption costing does therefore include the absorbed overheads in product costs and stock valuations. The way in which it operates means that in a large majority of cases there will be an **under- or over-recovery** of the overheads concerned. For example, in the case of an under-recovery of overheads, the overheads charged to the products or services will be less than the actual overheads paid out. To adjust this, the shortfall will have to be charged as an additional expense in the profit and loss account.

In the case of an over-recovery, too much will have been charged to the products or services and the difference will have to added back in the profit and loss account.

Mini-case: How to arrive at a quotation for a job using total absorption costing

Heylevel Ltd is a manufacturing company which has two production departments: Machining and Assembly, and two services departments: Power and Maintenance.

The estimated factory expenses for the quarter ending 31 December 20X6 are as follows:

Indirect Labour:	£000
Machining	40
Assembly	17.60
Power	79.40
Maintenance	24

Other costs:	
Supervision	12
Canteen	14.40
Rent and rates	50
Fuel and light	15
Machining	8.46
Assembly	0.84
Power	0.60
Maintenance	0.64
Plant insurance	3.76
Plant depreciation	46.50

The following additional information is available and is to be used, where appropriate, in apportioning the expenses to the departments:

	Machining	Assembly	Power	Maintenance
Floor area (sqm)	36,000	27,000	9,000	3,000
No. employees	80	120	30	10
Cost of plant	£600,000	£200,000	£100,000	£40,000
Plant annual (on cost) depreciation rates	20%	25%	10%	15%
Direct labour hours	3,880	15,120		
Machine hours	6,750	1,100		

Of the total power cost, 10% is charged to maintenance, and the remainder to the production departments on the basis of 30% machining and 70% to assembly.

The cost of the maintenance department is to be charged via technical estimates, 40% to machining department and 60% to assembly department.

We will now:

(a) prepare a departmental overhead distribution summary

(b) calculate the machine hour rate for the Machining Department, and a direct labour rate for the Assembly Department

(c) prepare a quotation for a job to which the following data relates:

Direct Material   £4,560

Direct Labour

Machining 5 hours @ £10 per hour
Assembly 8 hours @ £8 per hour

Machine hours 12 (in Machining Department)

Profit 40% on cost

(d) explain briefly why the figures in a) and b) are open to question.

Heylevel Limited
(a)

		Machin-ing	Assembly	Power	Mainte-nance	Total
Floor areas	a	36,000	27,000	9,000	3,000	75,000
Employees	b	80	120	30	10	240
Plant cost	c	600,000	200,000	100,000	40,000	940,000
Plant depreciation		20%	25%	10%	15%	
Direct Labour hours	d	3,880	15,120			19,000
Machine hours	e	6,750	1,100			7,850
	Basis					
Indirect	given					
Labour		40,000	17,600	79,400	24,000	161,000
Supervision	b	4,000	6,000	1,500	500	12,000
Canteen	b	4,800	7,200	1,800	600	14,400
Rent& rates	a	24,000	18,000	6,000	2,000	50,000
Fuel & light	a	7,200	5,400	1,800	600	15,000
Other costs	given	8,460	840	600	640	10,540
Plant ins.	c	2,400	800	400	160	3,760
Plant depr.	% cost/ 4	30,000	12,500	2,500	1,500	46,500
		120,860	68,340	94,000	30,000	313,200
Power	Est.	25,380	59,220	(94,000)	9,400	0
		146,240	127,560	0	39,400	313,200
Mtce.	Est.	15,760	23,640		(39,400)	0
Total costs		**£162,000**	**£151,200**	£0	£0	**£313,200**

(b) Divided by Direct Lab. hrs		15,120		
Machine hrs	6,750			
To get rate/hour	**£24.00**	**£10.00**		

(c)

	£	£
Direct materials (given)		4,560
Direct labour:		
Machining @ £10.00/hour – 5 hours	50	
Assembly @ £8.00/hour – 8 hours	<u>64</u>	114
Overheads:		
Machining @ £24.00/hour – 12 m/c hours	288	
Assembly @ £10.00 / hour – 8 hours	<u>80</u>	<u>368</u>
Total cost including overhead		**5,042**
Add mark-up @ 40% on cost (rounded to nearest £1)		<u>202</u>
Quotation		**£5,244**

Notes and comments

It might have been possible to apportion supervision over direct labour hours if the assumption were made that supervision is only applied to productive departments and most appropriately on the basis of workers' activity rather than a head-count. Plant insurance would in practice probably use a professional valuation done for insurance replacement purposes – here plant cost is the closest we can get to a 'value'. Depreciation is, of course, an allocation (not an apportionment) – based on the relevant depreciation rate and divided by four because we are only talking about a three month/quarter year period!

(d) The figures in parts (a) (b) and (c) are open to question for the following reasons:

- The overheads have to be estimated (pre-determined) before the process can commence. They could be reasonably accurate or way off course!
- The choice of the method of apportionment for those overheads which cannot be identified and traced to cost centres depend upon whosoever is doing the selecting! Which is the most appropriate for the type of expense is not always clear cut and open to debate.
- The allocated overheads, those which can be traced to cost centres, are still only estimated figures.
- There are a number of bases which can be used for dealing with service department costs. There are also a number of methods for dealing with service departments, some of which ignore services provided to other services departments!

- The number of machine hours or direct labour hours also have to be estimated and could prove to be way out! A lot of overheads vary more with time than output, so a time-based method is considered to be more appropriate than other methods.
- Thus, at the end of the period there could be an under or over-absorption (recovery) of overheads.
- Finally, there are the questions of whether or not administration overheads and/or selling and distribution overheads should have been included in the product cost.

A review of the solution, and spotting the catch (i.e. that the period was for one quarter of a year), illustrates that it was possible to calculate and allocate the depreciation, rather than having to use some arbitrary basis.
All we can do when we do have to apportion overheads is select the most appropriate base for the type of expense which is being dealt with.

Marginal costing

Definition

'The ascertainment of marginal costs and of the effect on profit of changes in volume or type of output by differentiating between **fixed costs and variable costs**'.

You should be aware that the marginal costing may also be described as variable costing, cost-volume-profit analysis, direct costing and differential costing.

Cost behaviour

The marginal costing system depends upon being able to divide costs between variable costs (i.e. marginal costs) and fixed costs, see Figures 18 and 19.

You should note that in marginal costing, fixed costs are treated as **period costs**. They are written off in the profit and loss account for the period to which they relate. They are not absorbed, i.e. included in cost of the product or service, and therefore, are not carried forward into the future as part of the stock valuations.

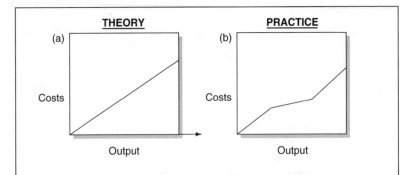

Figure 18 Variable costs – 'Vary with the level of activity (for example, direct materials and direct labour) within a relevant range'

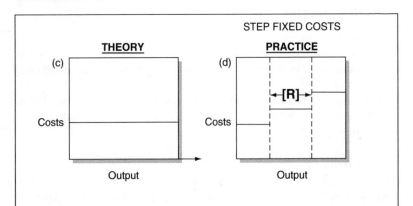

Figure 19 Fixed costs – those which remain unchanged irrespective of the level of activity (for example, rates, rents, salaries) within a relevant range (R)

The advantages of marginal costing

Some of the principal advantages claimed are:

- **Decision-making,** for example, the effect on future projects of changes in: demand, material prices, selling, prices, wage rates, product lines and selling methods, and so on; make or buy decisions; acceptance or rejection of an order at a price which is below the usual selling price; the discontinuance of a product or service; problems involving **limiting factors.**

- Fixed overheads do not distort profits, stocks, and so on.
- The use of the **contribution** and **profit volume ratio** (see below).

The disadvantages of marginal costing
However, there is also a downside, for example:

- If its use leads to 'cut throat' competition, for example, by reducing selling prices.
- As already mentioned, it is not always easy to separate overheads into their fixed and variable elements.

The marginal cost equation
You should find marginal costing arithmetic and marginal costing principles easy to follow. For more advanced problems, the arithmetic does become more complex, but the principles remain the same.

Mini-case: The marginal cost equation, an example

	Per unit	4000 units		% of sales
	£	£000		
Sales (S)	50	200		100
Less variable costs (VC)	30	120		60
Contribution (C)	20	80	(PV)	40
Less fixed costs (FC)		50		
Profit (P) (or Loss)		30		

Knowing any two of the figures sales, variable costs, contribution, fixed costs or the profit/loss enables us to work out one of the other figures. For example: S−VC = C; C−FC = P; C = FC + P and C + VC = S. This juggling around with the figures helps us to solve quite a number of marginal costing type problems.

The contribution indicated above contributes towards the recovery of the fixed overheads and then profit. The profit volume ratio of 40% (the PV ratio) is the contribution as a percentage of sales. This ratio tells us what the additional contribution would be from an additional increase in sales and can also be used to calculate the break-even point.

Mini-case: Changes in the selling price and where a profit target is set

The following data is used for this illustration:

$$\frac{\text{Contribution}}{\text{Sales}} \quad \text{e.g.} \quad \frac{80 \times 100 \text{ (as above)}}{200} = \textbf{40\%}$$

Sales £50 per unit; variable costs £30per unit; fixed costs £8,000; sale of 1000 units. We will use it to calculate and show:
(a) what the profit or loss amounts to, and
(b) what the position would be if the selling price was reduced by 10%, and
(c) using the selling price as in (b) above, how many units will have to be sold to produce the same profit as in (a) above.

(a)

	Per unit £	Per 1000 Units £
Sales	50	50,000
Less variable costs	*30*	*30,000*
Contribution	20	20,000
Less fixed costs		*8,000*
Profit		12,000

(b)

	Per unit £	Per 1000 units £
Sales (£50 less 10%)	45	45,000
Less variable costs	*30*	*30,000*
Contribution	15	15,000
Less fixed costs		*8,000*
Profit		7,000

(c)

Contribution needed = Fixed Costs plus profit target:
£8,000 + £12,000 = £20,000

The company must sell $\dfrac{\text{£20,000 Contribution needed}}{\text{£15 Contribution per unit}}$ = 1,333.3 units

---

Mini-case: Should we discontinue to produce and sell product I?

The Estelle Ramillon Co. Ltd produces three products. The following information has been extracted from last year's accounts:

	W £000	I £000	K £000
Sales	650	500	320
Variable cost	340	330	220
Fixed cost	240	100	70

In addition further research has indicated that the sales of product I are likely to be £400,000 next year due to competitive pressures, and its variable costs £300,000.The sales and costs of the other two products are expected to be the same next year. The fixed costs were shared out using a total absorption costing approach and are expected to be the same in the next year.

The Managing Director calls for immediate withdrawal of product I from the product range.

By dropping product I, fixed costs would be reduced by £25,000. We will look at this scenario in three parts using a marginal costing approach, as follows:

(a) to show last year's position, and
(b what the position would be if:
   i   product I is not withdrawn
   ii product I is withdrawn, and
(c) to comment on our findings.

Estelle Ramillon Co. Ltd.
(a)

	W £000	I £000	K £000	Total £000
Sales	650	500	320	1,470
Less variable costs	340	330	220	890
Contribution	210	170	100	580
Less fixed costs				410
Profit				170

(b)

i) If product I is not withdrawn

	W £000	I £000	K £000	Total £000
Sales	650	400	320	1,370
Less variable costs	340	300	220	860
Contribution	310	100	100	510
Less fixed costs				410
Profit				100

ii) If product I is withdrawn

	W £000	I £000	K £000	Total £000
Contribution (As above)	310	Withdrawn	100	410
Less fixed costs (410 less 25 = 385)				385
Profit				25

(c)

You can observe that product I, given the revised information is making a contribution towards the recovery of the fixed overheads of £100,000. If it is withdrawn this contribution would be lost, offset by the saving of £25,000 in the fixed costs i.e. a net reduction of £75,000. Management should be advised that their absorption costing approach is just a method designed to attempt to recover their overheads. Its use cannot lead to accurate/realistic product costs because of the way in which overheads are apportioned to cost centres etc. Product I should not be discontinued. If it was discontinued profits would fall from £100,000 to £25,000!

The limiting factor

When a factor is of such importance that it influences all the other budgets, it is a limiting factor and must always be taken into account before all the other budgets are prepared. It dictates what can and cannot be done i.e. it constrains the activities of the company/organization.

Limiting (key) factors – some examples

- Supply – raw materials, finished goods
- Demand – sales demand

- Labour supply
- Production capacity
- Warehouse capacity
- Finance
- Government – restrictions, and so on.

The simplified mini-case which follows, should help you to understand the technique which can be used to resolve the limiting/key factor problems. The aim is to maximize the contribution per unit of the limiting factor, for example, contribution per hour, contribution per minute, contribution per kilo, contribution per litre, and so on.

Mini-case: A limiting factor is a problem

Materials are limited in supply to 1,000 kilos per period, a choice must be made between producing Product A and Product B, details of which are:

	Product A	Product B
	£	£
Selling price per unit	300	200
Variable cost per unit	100	120
Material required for one unit	4 Kilos	1 Kilo

The solution to this problem can be found using the contribution per unit of the limiting factor, which in this case is the kilos of materials which are available.

	Product A	Product B
	£	£
Contribution (S–VC)	200	80
Contribution per unit of the limiting factor (*Divide by the kilos required to produce the product*)	50 per kilo	80 per kilo

If we multiply the contribution per kilo by the supply of materials above, the maximum contributions possible will be:

Product A	Product B
£50,000	£80,000

By recognizing that there is a limiting/key factor at work, switching to producing and selling product B could generate a £30,000 more than the contribution which could be achieved by producing and selling product A.

Break-even analysis

The break-even point is the point at which costs and revenues are equal, or put another way, the point at which the contribution is exactly equal to the fixed costs.

How to calculate the break-even point

Fixed costs divided by the PV ratio = the break-even point. The profit/volume ratio was described earlier in this section and is the contribution as a percentage of sales.

For example, where fixed costs are £24,000 and the profit/volume ratio is 60%, the break-even point would be:

$$£24,000 \text{ fixed costs} \times \frac{100}{60} = \textbf{£40,000} \quad \text{or} \quad \frac{\text{Fixed costs} \times \text{sales}}{\text{Sales} - \text{variable costs}}$$

$$\text{or} \quad \frac{\text{Fixed costs}}{\text{Contribution per unit}} = \text{Break-even point in units}$$

The break-even point in units can be converted to a value by multiplying it by the selling price per unit.

Mini-case: How to calculate the break-even point

The break-even point can therefore be calculated, for example using the formula, fixed costs divided by the profit volume (PV) ratio, as follows:

	£000
Fixed costs	200
Sales	540
Variable costs	360

	£000
Sales	540
Less variable costs	360
Contribution	180

The PV ratio is:

$$\frac{180}{540} \times 100 = 33.333\%$$

The break-even point is:

$$£200 \text{ (fixed costs)} \times \frac{100}{33.333} = £600.006$$

Break-even charts

The relationship between Sales, Costs and Profit can be displayed by using a break-even chart.

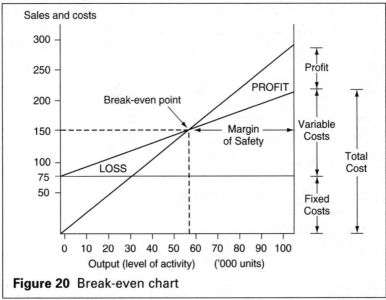

Figure 20 Break-even chart

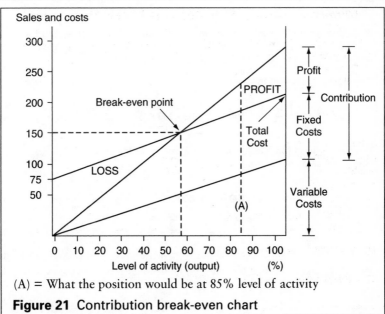

(A) = What the position would be at 85% level of activity

Figure 21 Contribution break-even chart

Mini-case: A break-even and profit target puzzle

Chehoi plc operates two stores, Ruffles and Changwai. From the data given below we will attempt to calculate:

(a) each store's break-even point, and
(b) the sales required in each case to achieve a target net profit 10% of the capital invested.

	Ruffles	**Changwai**
Fixed costs	£200,000	£480,000
Profit/Volume ratio	60%	40%
Capital invested	£12million	£20million

(a) We can compute the break-even points, as follows:

Ruffles   **Changwai**

$$£200,000 \times \frac{100}{60} = £333,333 \qquad £480,000 \times \frac{100}{40} = £1,200,000$$

(b) The contribution needed to produce a profit target of 10% of the capital invested can be worked out, as follows:

	Ruffles **£000**	**Changwai** **£000**
Fixed costs	200	480
plus profit target	1,200	2,000
Contribution	£1,400	£2,480

You know what the profit volume ratio is for each of the stores, and this is the key to working out the sales required to achieve the profit targets.
The contribution for Ruffles represents 60% of the sales.

Therefore, sales need to be: (£000)

$$\frac{£1,400}{60} \times 100 = £2,333.333$$

The contribution for Changwai represents 40% of the sales.
Therefore, sales need to be: (£000)

$$\frac{£2,480}{40} \times 100 = £6,200$$

The aim of the above was to ensure that you understand the relationship between the figures which together make up the marginal cost equation.

The limitations of break-even analysis

There are a number of limitations associated with break-even analysis, and some of the principal ones are listed below.

- As output rises it does not follow that there will be a proportionate increase in sales.
- Fixed costs may change at different levels of output/activity, for example, an increase in fixed costs could be necessary to support an increase in the level of activity.
- Variable costs and total sales income (sales) may not be a straight line.
- The time span affects the chart.
- Management decisions can affect both fixed and variable costs, for example, expanding operations.
- The product-mix cannot be predicted with accuracy.
- Selling prices may have to vary in order to sell more (for example, to different markets/customers).
- Efficiency is not always constant.

KEY WORDS

Identified and traced	Allocated
Apportioned	Equitable basis
Absorption rates	Recovery rates
Machine hours	Direct labour hours
Under- or over-recovery	Fixed and variable costs
Period costs	Decision making
Limiting factors	Contribution
Profit volume ratio	Break-even analysis

Further reading

Chadwick, L., Chapters 3 & 4 *Management Accounting*, Thomson Learning, 1998.

Drury, C., Chapter 8 *Costing an Introduction*, Thomson Learning, 1998.

Upchurch, A., Chapters 5 & 6 *Management Accounting Principles and Practice*, Financial Times Prentice Hall, 1998.

Essay topics and assignments

1. Describe and illustrate the principal differences between total absorption costing and marginal costing. [25 marks]

2. Discuss the drawbacks and problems which are associated with the total absorption costing approach for dealing with overheads. [25 marks]

Data response question

You have been provided with the following budgeted overheads which relate to the forthcoming period for Almondbury plc:

	£000
Rent and rates	80
Light and heat	50
Welfare and canteen	40
Insurance of buildings	20
Insurance of machinery	12
Works manager's salary	36

Department	Indirect Labour	Depreciation of machinery/equipment	Other overheads allocation
	£000	£000	£000
L	50	40	16
E	24	28	10
S	22	12	6
Power	32	8	5
Stores	30	4	3
	158	92	40

You are also provided with the following additional information:

	L	E	S	Power	Stores
No. of employees	4	16	2	2	2
Floor area (sq metres)	300	200	100	100	300
Replacement value of machinery and equipment	£000	£000	£000	£000	£000
	400	64	40	48	32
Use of stores (%)	20	40		15	
Use of power	60	30	10	–	–
Machine hours	100,000	12,000	–	–	–
Direct labour hours	16,000	40,000	20,000	–	–

Required:

(a) prepare a departmental overhead distribution summary, and [12 marks]

(b) calculate the overhead absorption rates using a machine hour rate for departments L, and direct labour rate for departments E and S

[3 marks]

(c) using the following data prepare a quotation for job 007XL5 [4 marks]

Direct material	£5,850
Direct labour:	
Department L	20 hours @£15
Department E	12 hours @ £12
Department S	10 hours @ £10
Mark up @	40% on cost
Department L	60 machine hours

(d) comment on the validity of the methods of apportionment which were used in Part (a) above. [6 marks]

Chapter Nine

Budgets and standards

'We just look at the figures and add 6%.'
'No one consults us.'
'If we overspend so what.'
'It is simply imposed from above.'
'I go to the buying office for a standard price, and they just pull a figure out of a hat.'
Leslie Chadwick, comments from Chapter 12 'Budgets – Why ignore good practice?' in *Myths and Realities of Managerial Accounting and Finance*, Pitman Financial Times, 1998.

Introduction

We now move on to budgetary control, a topic area which affects all of us, both at home and at work. We are particularly concerned with budgeting in a business environment. Budgetary control is of prime importance to both public and private sector organizations. It is one of management accounting's most important topic areas.

CIMA (The Chartered Institute of Management Accountants) provides us with some clear concise definitions which should provide you with an insight into what budgeting and budgetary control involves, three of which are as follows:

A budget

A plan expressed in money. It is prepared and approved prior to the budget period and may show income, expenditure, and the capital to be employed. May be drawn up showing incremental effects on former budgeted or actual figures, or be compiled by zero-based budgeting.

Budget centre

A section of an entity for which control may be exercised and budgets prepared.

Budgetary control

The establishment of budgets relating the **responsibilities** of executives to the requirements of a **policy,** and the **continuous comparison** of actual with budgeted results, either to secure by individual **action** the **objectives** of that policy or to provide a basis for its revision. (This is a very good and very useful definition, containing many important keywords).

The household budget

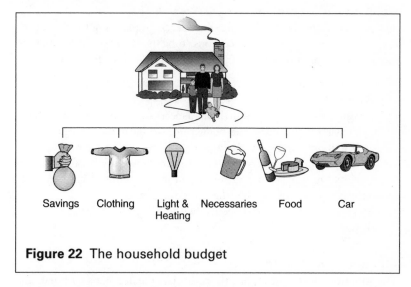

Savings   Clothing   Light &   Necessaries   Food   Car
                       Heating

Figure 22 The household budget

Source: L. Chadwick, *Essential Management Accounting for Managers,* Financial Times Prentice Hall, 2001.

Our introduction to this most important area starts with a review of the household budget as illustrated in Figure 22. The principles which we can deduce from a review of the household budget also relate to both public and private sector organizations.

There needs to be:

- a **common sense** approach, for example, setting realistic targets
- **co-ordination,** for example, a budget committee, a timetable for meetings
- careful **planning** of policy and objectives, for example, market share, return on capital employed, green issues etc.
- comparison of the actual and budgeted figures, for example, sales budgets, expenditure budgets. This will provide an **early warning** of those areas which are not going according to plan
- a budget controller to organize, co-ordinate and **communicate.** Such a person would need 'people skills' in addition to a knowledge of finance and accounting. They have to secure the co-operation and full participation of all those who are involved in the preparation process and the implementation process.

The benefits of budgeting

Planning and co-ordination

Success in business is closely related to success in planning for the future. Planning enables the need for decisions to be made early and for them to focus on the overall objectives. In this context, the budget:

- provides a formal planning framework, and insists that planning does take place!
- co-ordinates the various individual aspects of the business by providing a master plan (the **master budget**) for the business as a whole. This is particularly important in a large organization engaged in producing several different products or services. Otherwise, it is all too easy for individual managers to concentrate on their own personal objectives or their perceptions of what the objectives are!
- provides a framework of objectives within which later decisions can be taken.

Authorizing and delegating

The adoption of a budget explicitly **authorizes** the decisions within it, and reduces the need to continuously ask top management to make decisions. The responsibility for carrying out the decisions is **delegated** to individual managers.

Evaluating performance

It provides a score card, for example, has the salesperson done very well or very badly? By setting targets for them to achieve, the budget provides a benchmark against which their performance can be assessed.

You should note that before a budget can successfully be used for this purpose, it must be accepted as being fair and reasonable by all those who are responsible for carrying it out.

Identification of trends

It is important that management should be made aware as soon as possible of any new **trends**, whether in relation to demand or marketing, and so on. The budget, by providing specific expectations with which actual performance is continuously compared, provides a mechanism for the earlier detection of any unexpected trends.

Communication and motivation

The budget communicates at two levels. The preparation stage involves communication between top management and various other levels of management about objectives and the ways of achieving them. Secondly, after it has been prepared and approved, it communicates the objectives of the firm from the management.

Control

Having set its objectives (goals), management uses the budget to **monitor** and **control** the running of the business. By continuously comparing actual with planned results, deviations are readily noted and appropriate corrective action taken. There is, however, a danger in adhering to the budget too rigidly. Circumstances may change, and the budget should therefore change accordingly.

Budgetary control is in effect an early warning system. Comparisons of budgeted and actual figures take place at regular intervals, for example, monthly, quarterly. **Variances** are computed, reported and acted upon.

Variances can be adverse (A) or favourable (F).

(Extract) **Budget and actual comparative statement**
[Details of purpose, etc.] Date.........

Item	Actual	Budget	Variance	Reason for the variance

Note that the above could also include last year's details for comparative purposes.

Figure 23 A comparative budget and actual statement

In reporting the variances, those which are considered to be significant, and the reasons why they have occurred, should be highlighted on the budget and actual comparative statement, Figure 23. This will enable management to focus on those high priority items which really need their time and attention, and to sort out appropriate corrective action. This highlighting of variances system can be described as **management by exception**.

Rules for effective budgeting

Budgets must be accepted as a management planning technique. (The accountant collects and collates the data.) They need to be built up by areas of responsibility, i.e. control by responsibility/responsibility accounting, for example, an individual manager could be responsible for the sales target for a particular sales area.

All those responsible must **participate** in setting budgets, i.e. budgets

---

Mini-case: Why not ask the workers?

The Happy Study plc involved worker representatives on several of its budget planning committees. Lol Poppins, the production manager, was certain that the milling department could quite easily achieve the production target which was being proposed. The worker representative explained to the meeting why this would be impossible, and saved the company from a major embarrassment and from losing a vast sum of money!

---

should not be imposed from above, this can involve all levels of management and worker representation.

Those responsible for setting and implementing the budget must understand the objectives. This requires education on a continuing basis and

---

Mini-case: Sky high targets

Sky Walker Cars Co. Ltd set their sales targets so high that it was almost impossible for sales staff to earn any bonus. This had a de-motivating effect, some staff just gave up trying to meet their targets, others voted with their feet and went to work elsewhere. This meant that the company had a very high rate of labour turnover, which can be very expensive, for example, in terms of recruitment and selection costs, induction and training costs.

---

effective communication. The goals and targets which are set should be realistic, fair and reasonable.

Budgets must be co-ordinated, monitored and reviewed, for example, watch for changes in the **basic assumptions** on which they were based such as: the rate of inflation, changes in interest rates, pay settlements, oil prices, international problems, and so on. Approval of budgets must be specifically communicated down the line to indicate management acceptance as a basis for control, i.e. management in action. Control must be by flexible budgets. A flexible budget is one which is designed to change with the level of output or level of activity.

The reported actuals must match the budgeted content if comparison is to be valid. It is not unknown for a company to work out the budget one way, and then to work out the actuals using a different formula! Control should be directed towards significant exceptions, i.e. management by exception. This is in line with the process of highlighting the significant adverse variances on the budget and actual comparative statements.

Control should be directed towards action rather than recrimination. The cost of the systems must not exceed the value obtained, i.e. cost/benefit. Finally **behavioural factors** should not be ignored.

Mini-case: The 'whizkid'

Once upon a time there was a University Head of Department (I must add, not from the University where I am employed). This particular individual was so wise and knew so much (or so he thought), that he did not see the need to consult his staff concerning the purchase of very expensive high-tech equipment. Unknown to him, his staff were in effect 'laughing behind his back' and commenting to each other about the shock that was about to descend. Not one of them was prepared to point out the folly of it all to the 'whiz-kid' because he had not consulted them. He had in fact insulted them by his failure to consult. When the equipment arrived, it could not be used, without first buying additional expensive peripheral equipment. The current year's budget had been used up, so the additional equipment could not be purchased until the next year out of that year's budget.
The moral. Why not consult, rather than insult!

The above mini-case does illustrate how behavioural aspects can come into play. The way in which budgets are prepared and used do affect the way in which individuals within the system behave, for example, targets and the effect on motivation, and perceptions where communications are unclear.

Cash budgets (cash flow forecasts)

What is a cash budget?

It is important to remember that income and expenditure as recorded for profit measurement purposes are usually not the same as the cash receipts and payments. This is particularly obvious in the case of expenditure on fixed assets where large sums of cash can be paid in one period and then written off for profit measurement purposes over future periods by way of depreciation.

Another example is the time lag between buying or selling goods on credit and paying/receiving the cash.

You should note that the **cash flow forecast**, (the alternative name for the **cash budget**) is not the same as the cash flow statement which is published in the reports and accounts of companies.

The purpose of a cash budget

The principal purpose of a cash budget (cash flow forecast) is to:

- make sure that cash is available when needed
- highlight cash shortages
- highlight cash surpluses.

There are a number of uses to which the cash budget (cash-flow budget) can be put, it can be used:

- as an aid to management in controlling its cash resources for example, the **treasury function** which involves the investment of surplus cash, on a short-term basis such as 24 hours, one week or one month
- as an aid in monitoring performance in areas where cash control is an important performance indicator, for example, credit control, which attempts to ensure that cash from debtors is collected in an efficient manner
- as a control device to enable changes in plans or remedial action to be taken to correct an outcome which initially looks as if it will be unsatisfactory or unacceptable
- as a discussion document in obtaining third party co-operation in project implementation, for example, with banks and other lending institutions where financing facilities are being sought, or to support internal applications for limited resources

Profit does not equal cash over any given period. A profitable business can be problematic because of the time taken in collecting the cash, which puts severe strain on cash flow. It is important, therefore, to know if and when these cash demands may be made on a business: hence, the need to forecast.

The cash graph

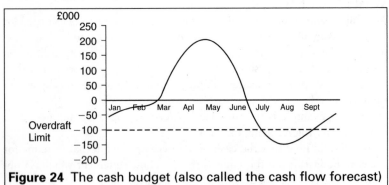

Figure 24 The cash budget (also called the cash flow forecast)

From a review of the cash graph, Figure 24, you should note that the critical position occurs when the cash flow falls below the overdraft limit. The position will have been identified well in advance of its estimated occurrence. Thus, corrective action can be taken in good time to avoid the situation.

We will now go through Comdot Software Ltd. a step by step example which illustrates how we produce a master budget which consists of: a cash budget, a budgeted profit and loss account, and a budgeted balance sheet.

Comdot Software Ltd

Com and Dot are starting up a new business, Comdot Software Ltd. on 1 January 20X4 and have provided us with the following information:

	£
Quaterly rent of premises	3,000
(First payment due on 1st Jan.)	
Cash outlay on equipment - payable 15 January	200,000
Cash outlay on equipment - payable 16 May	40,000
Monthly planned purchases of stock for re-sale	
January	10,000
February	12,000
March to June (per month)	20,000

All stock is bought on two months' credit

For example January's purchase is estimated to be paid for in March

Monthly planned sales are:	
January	6,000
February	18,000
March to June (per Month)	36,000

- All sales are on one month's credit.
- The monthly cash outlay on general expenses is expected to be £5,000. Salaries are expected to be £4,000 per month.
- Depreciation of equipment on the first half year is computed at £12,000.
- On 1 Jan. 20X4 Com and Dot will provide £100,000 Ordinary Share Capital to the business and their bankers will provide them with a long-term loan of £200,000.

- The budgeted closing stock at the end of June, 20X4 is estimated at £16,000.

The method of going about this task is described and illustrated below.

1. To complete the cash budget we firstly pick up the opening balance, in Comdot Software Ltd's case the £300,000 start-up capital.
2. Next we pick up the sales, then the purchases taking into account the periods of credit given/taken.
3. We then pick up all the other expenses plotting them in the month in which they are to be paid out.
4. Having inserted all the data the next step is to start and balance each month starting with January. The closing balance for January becomes the opening balance for February, and so on.

The Comdot Software Ltd illustration provides you with a very good way of appreciating the difference between profit and cash. All you have to do is contrast the cash budget with the budgeted profit and loss account.

Projected profit and loss account for the six months to June 30 20X4

Comdot Software Ltd	£	£
Sales		168,000
Cost of sales:		
Purchases	102,000	
Less closing stock	(16,000)	
		86,000
Gross Profit		**82,000**
Expenses:		
Rent	6,000	
Salaries	24,000	
General expenses	30,000	
Depreciation	12,000	
		72,000
Net Profit		**£10,000**

Comdot Software Ltd			Time lag 1 month	Time lag 2 months		Cash budget		
Month 20X4	Balance b/f £000	Capital £000	Sales £000	Purchases £000	Rent £000	General Rent Salaries £000	Fixed Assets £000	Balance c/f £000
Jan		300			3	9	200	88
Feb	88		6			9		85
Mar	85		18	10		9		84
Apr	84		36	12	3	9		96
May	96		36	20		9	40	63
Jun	63		36	20		9		70
			+Debtors 36	+Creditors 40	6	54	240	
			168	102			12	
			Total Sales	Total Purchases		Depreciation	228	
						Net book value		

Figure 25 The cash budget

Projected balance sheet at June 30, 20X4

Comdot Software Ltd	£	£
Fixed assets:		
Equipment at cost		240,000
Less Accumulated depreciation		12,000
		228,000
Working capital (Net current assets):		
Current assets:		
Stock	16,000	
Debtors *(credit period one month)*	36,000	
Cash *(as per the Cash budget)*	70,000	
	122,000	
Current liabilities:		
Creditors *(credit period two months)*	40,000	82,000
		310,000
Capital Employed		
Ordinary share capital		100,000
Retained earnings *(per the Profit and loss account)*		10,000
		110,000
Long-term loan		200,000
		£310,000

The budgeted profit and loss account illustrated above is made up of the totals extracted from the adjusted cash budget, depreciation information, the closing stock figure, and so on. When we compare the cash budget with the budgeted profit and loss account, it provides us with a reasonable understanding as to why cash and profits are different. When you earn profits you may spend all or some of it.

The realization concept dictates the treatment of the sales/purchases for the purpose of computing the profit or loss. Stock will appear in the cash budget purchases figure when the purchases concerned are paid for, but will only become an expense for profit and loss purposes when it is consumed and sold. Depreciation is a non-cash item, the cash moves when the fixed asset concerned is paid for.

Finally, you need to remember that cash is recorded in the cash budget when it moves in or out. For example, it does not matter about the period of time covered by a dividend paid or received, or rent paid or received, what matters is when it is going to be paid or received.

	Cash budget	Profit and loss account
Sales	included in the month in which the cash is received	all sales included whether or not the cash has been received
Purchases	included in the month in which it is paid out	all purchases included whether or not the cash has been paid out
Opening and closing stocks	not included	accounted for in computing the gross profit
Expenses without any period of credit	included	included
Depreciation	not included	included as an expense

Figure 26 Cash and profits – a contrast

Mini-case: A cash budgeting system forces management into action

The cash budget preparation process in itself will dictate that management will have to think about the future. They will have to organize meetings, the collection and analysis of relevant data, prepare and ensure that there are timetables, and careful co-ordination, co-operation, and good clear communications. This should involve the participation of appropriate personnel so that their views can be registered and discussed. Budgets are inter-related and so they cannot be prepared in isolation. The cash budget will draw on the information provided by the sales budget, the production budget, the purchasing budget, the capital expenditure and many others, hence the need for meetings and effective co-ordination.

Management will need to delegate authority and responsibility for the cash budget and its component parts to various members of staff, 'control by responsibility'. This would include their roles in the preparation process and their authority, for example, re the implementation and control process.

Management will know at the preparation stage if action is called for in terms of exceeding the overdraft or having surplus cash to invest short term, or if cash is not available when it is needed and take appropriate action.

The frequent comparisons and reporting of budgeted and actual figures provides an 'early warning system'. Management are forced into action to remedy adverse effects as and when they arise.

Thus, sound cash management should include making good use of cash budgets and force management into action. Such action is essential if they are to realise the objectives which they themselves have set, and if they are to survive and prosper in the long-term. However such budgets are only estimates based on the best available information at the time of their preparation. If the assumptions on which they were based change significantly, then the cash budget must also be changed. If this is not done, management may be faced with a number of behavioural and motivational problems.

Flexible budgets

Fixed budget A budget which is designed to remain unchanged irrespective of the level of activity actually attained.

Flexible budget A budget which, by recognizing the difference between fixed, semi-variable and variable costs, is designed to change in relation to the level of activity attained.

Here is an example of a flexible budget. You should note that in order to prepare one, we have to separate costs into their fixed and variable elements. Also, observe how the fixed costs remain the same up to a sales level of £130,000 and then there is an increase of £4,000 i.e. a step in the fixed costs.

MONTHLY DEPARTMENTAL FLEXIBLE BUDGET

	£000	£000	£000	£000	£000
Sales	<u>100</u>	<u>110</u>	<u>120</u>	<u>130</u>	<u>140</u>
Direct costs					
(e.g. Finished goods, wages)	24	27	30	33	36
Variable overheads	8	9	10	11	12
Semi-variable overheads	5	6	7	8	9
Fixed overheads	15	15	15	15	19 (Step)
	—	—	—	—	—
	<u>52</u>	<u>57</u>	<u>62</u>	<u>67</u>	<u>76</u>
Profit	48	53	58	63	64

Budgets can lead to a 'blinkered approach' by departmental executives, for example, they may want to achieve their personal objectives at all costs, regardless of the effect upon the welfare of the whole organization.

One should remember that budgets intend to influence human behaviour and, as such, will inevitably create human responses and, since one cannot always predict human behaviour, problems will arise. This necessitates a constant monitoring and review of the budgetary system by top management to ensure that behavioural malfunctions are quickly noted and dealt with.

Zero base budgeting

Zero base budgeting (ZBB) is a budgeting system in which all the budgets start from 'scratch'. It has been found to be particularly useful for dealing with services and projects which involve capital expenditure. The staff concerned have to justify, rank and prioritize the services and projects. The aim being to bring about a much fairer and better way of distributing the scarce resources of the company/organization.

Standard costing

Standard costing involves setting standard quantities and standard prices for the elements of cost. For materials, the standard quantity of materials which goes into the product e.g. parts to make motor components, or the mix of chemicals needed to produce the product, has to be predetermined, and so does the standard price of the materials. With labour, standard times for performing various production operations have to be established, for example, by using work study techniques, and standard labour rates of pay have also to be estimated. Standard rates have also to be calculated for the overheads.

Control is carried out by comparing actual performance with the predetermined standard, and then reporting the variances to management. They can then consider what form of corrective action will be the most effective response.

KEY WORDS

Responsibilities	Policy
Continuous comparison	Action
Objectives	Common sense
Co-ordination	Planning
Early warning	Communication
Master budget	Authorization
Delegation	Trends
Monitor	Control
Variances	Management by exception
Participation	Behavioural factors
Basic assumptions	Treasury function
Cash budgets (cash flow forecasts)	Flexible budgets
Fixed budgets	Standard costing
Zero base budgeting (ZBB)	

Further reading

Chadwick, L., Chapters 7 and 8 *Management Acccounting*, International Thomson Business Press, 1998.

Drury, C., Chapters 13 and 15 *Costing An Introduction*, International Thomson Learning, 1998.

Dyson, J.R., Chapters 15 and 16 *Accounting for Non-Accounting Students*, Financial Times Prentice Hall, 2001.

Upchurch, A., Chapters 13 and 14 *Management Accounting, Principles and Practice*, Financial Times Prentice Hall, 1998.

Useful website

For management accounting principles and practice
www.ftmanagement.com

Essays and assignments

1. In relation to budgeting and budgetary control, explain and illustrate the importance of:

   - control by responsibility [6 marks]
   - management by exception [6 marks]
   - participation [6 marks]
   - the early warning system. [7 marks]

2. Describe how the budget preparation process and budgetary control can cause behavioural and motivational problems. [25 marks]

Data response questions

1   Read the extract and answer **all** parts of the question which follows

(a) Complete the cash flow forecast (attached) for Scunpool United's next season. [9 marks]

   (b) Scunpool United is not a profitable business. Examine the circumstances in which any business can survive without profits. [8 marks]

   (c) Evaluate ways in which Scunpool United could improve its cash flow. [9 marks]

SCUNPOOL UNITED

Scunpool United Football Club is a small club playing in the lower reaches of the Third Division of the Football League. The club is not a profitable business and gate money is falling as spectators prefer to stay at home and watch the Premier League on television.

The club's accountant has drawn up a cash flow forecast for the season ahead.

All of the following forecast figures of cash inflows and outflows are based on last season.

The club plays twenty matches at home per season and expects an average crowd of 3000, with each spectator paying £8 per match. The club also expects to reach the second round of two cup competitions and to receive a total of £50 000 gate money from these matches.

Other receipts come from a club lottery and anticipated income for the season is £50 000.

Additional income, estimated at £90 000 for the season, is derived from selling advertising around the ground and in match day programmes.

Expenditures on match days is budgeted at £5 000 per match and for cup matches there has to be extra policing, increasing the budgeted total cup expenditure to a total of £30 000.

The biggest costs to the club, however, are the players' wages which are based on a 17-man squad earning an average of £25 000 per season. Other staff wages per season amount to £80 000. The manager, Kevin Smith, earns £50 000 per season.

The ground needs urgent maintenance to meet the local council's Health and Safety standards and £80 000 has to be set aside for this before the season starts.

Other overheads include insurance, heating and telephone bills. This additional expenditure adds up to £20 000 over the season.

Variable costs include the production of the match day programmes and certain ground staff who are paid on match days only. The club has an overdraft limit of £500 000 and the current overdraft is £200 000. The great hope is that one of the younger players is snapped up by All Star United, a Premier League team.

Adapted from AQA Q2, Unit 1, Specimen Paper, 2000

ATTACHMENT TO ASSESSMENT UNIT
Cash Flow Forecast for Scunpool United Football Club

Cash In: £

Gate money	
Cup revenue	50 000
Club lottery	50 000
Advertisements and programme sales	90 000
Total cash inflow	

Cash Out:

Match day expenditure	
Policing	30 000
Wages	425 000
Other staff	80 000
Manager	50 000
Ground maintenance	80 000
Other	20 000
Total cash inflow	

Net cash flow	
Opening bank balance	
Closing bank balance	

Chapter Ten

Capital investment appraisal

Which cash flows should we use, and how can we forecast them?
What are relevant (incremental) cash flow?
How can we take taxation into account?
Which discount rate should we use?
Which cost of capital should we use?
How do we account for risk and uncertainty?
Which method of capital investment appraisal should we use?
The above represent some of the most frequently asked questions relating to capital investment appraisal.

Capital investment appraisal, an introduction

Capital investment appraisal is nowadays described in many companies as project appraisal. It is a very important part of financial management, as it enables management to compare different projects which extend over a number of years. There are a number of methods which can be used, those which take into account the **time value of money** and those methods which do not take the time value of money into account.

The methods which use the time value of money are based on the idea that £1 today will be worth less in the future. They make use in particular of the **present value** of £1 table. For example, if we look at the present value of £1 table, 10% rate, the first five year's figures are as follows:

Period/year	10% discount rate
1	0.909
2	0.826
3	0.751
4	0.683
5	0.621

They tell us what the present value of £1 will be in one, two, three, four or five years' time. For example, the present value of £1 receivable in five years' time is £0.621 (i.e. around 62p). We just multiply the amount which we need to discount by the appropriate discount rate. For example, the present value of £2,000 receivable in 3 years' time, at a discount rate of

10%, is £2,000 × 0.751 = £1,502. Put another way, the present value tables tell us that if we invest £1,502 now at 10% compound interest, in three years' time it would amount to £2,000.

The cash flows which are used tend to be the **relevant (incremental) cash flows.** You should however, note at the outset that the financial information provided by the various methods is only one component part of the decision-making process, for example, certain non-financial factors have also to be taken into account.

Relevant (incremental) cash flows

The relevant cash flows have to be estimated using historic information updated by the best available information about the future. There are simple rules which can be applied to assess whether or not a cash flow is relevant. The rules are as follows:

- If the cash flow happens whether or not the project goes ahead, it is irrelevant. For example, certain fixed costs will have to be paid whatever happens, existing employees who are moved to work on the project would still have to be paid if the project goes ahead and if the project does not go ahead.
- If the cash flow happens, only if the project goes ahead, it is a relevant cash flow, for example, if as a direct consequence of a project going ahead salaries have to be paid to new members of staff, or additional fixed costs such as rent have to be paid out.
- **Depreciation** is not a relevant cash flow, because it is a non-cash item. The cash moves when the fixed asset in question is paid for.
- **Opportunities lost** as a result of a project going ahead are relevant. For example, if an existing machine or equipment is traded in for £20,000, to acquire a new machine costing £320,000 the relevant cost would be £300,000, i.e. cost less the trade-in. If the machine which has been traded in would have been disposed of in year 4 of the project for £6,000, the disposal value is a relevant cost of year 4, because it represents a lost opportunity, i.e. if the project did not go ahead, the company would receive the £6,000 in year 4. If the project does go ahead the company loses £6,000 in year 4. The disposal value on the new machine, if any, to be received at the end of the project would be a relevant receipt.

Evaluation methods

Methods based on the financial accounting figures

There are quite a number of profitability ratios which look at the **return on capital employed** (**ROCE**). This may also be described as the return on investment (ROI).

For capital investment appraisal purposes we have to estimate the accounting profits for the lifetime of the project, and this does involve taking depreciation into account.

The payback method

This method looks at how long it takes for the project to cover the amount which has been invested in the project. For example, a project investment at the start of £24,000 generates relevant cash flows of £6,000 for six years. The payback is 4 years, i.e. the cumulative cash flows at the end of year 4 will be £24,000 which is equal to the amount invested.

This method is simple to understand. Its major drawback is that it does not take the time value of money into account.

Discounted cash flow (DCF) methods

There tends to be general agreement by those who are involved in capital investment appraisal that those methods that take into account the time value of money are to be preferred.

Mini-case: The evaluation of capital investment projects (an illustration of the various methods)

A proposed project which involves the purchase of computers and software for £80,000 has had its relevant cash in-flows estimated to be as follows:

Year	1	2	3	4	5
(all £000)	20	24	32	30	18

The company's cost of capital is 10%.
The computers and software are to be written off at 20% on cost per annum, and will have no residual/scrap value at the end of their life.

Note that in this particular case and many others, companies use their cost of capital as the discount rate. Capital investment appraisal methods which use the time value of money are also referred to as **discounted cash flow** (**DCF**) techniques. The above mini-case figures will now be used to illustrate the methods which do take into account the time value of money.

The net present value method

Year	Relevant cash flow	Discount factor @ 10%	Present value of cash flows £000
1	20	0.909	18.180
2	24	0.826	19.824
3	32	0.751	24.032
4	30	0.683	20.490
5	18	0.621	11.178
			93.704
Less the initial investment in the computers etc. at the start			80,000
= The net present value of the project			£13.704

After the discounting process, the positive **net present value** (**NPV**) is an indication that the project is wealth-creating and worthy of further consideration.

Note that the net present value is the present value of the cash flows less the initial investment at the start of the project. The start of the project may also be described as year 0. The reason for this is that at the start of the project the present value of £1 is £1.

The discounted payback method

From the above, we can work out the discounted payback. This will take place when the cumulative present value cash flows are equal to the initial investment. A quick review reveals that this happens towards the end of year 4. We can work it out, as follows:

Years 1 to 3: cumulative £62,036. This is £17,964 short of the £80,000 initial investment. Assuming that the cash flows are spread evenly throughout the year, it would take:

$$\frac{£17,964}{£20,490} \times 12 \text{ months} = 10.36 \text{ months}$$

The discounted payback is around 3 years 10 months. By taking into account the time value of money it does improve upon the payback method which uses the unadjusted cash flows.

The internal rate of return method (IRR)

The **internal rate of return** is the discount rate which will give a net present value of nil, i.e. the rate at which the discounted cash flows are equal to the initial investment. In order to find the IRR for the above project, we need to compute a positive NPV: this we have already done at the 10% rate which works out at £13,704. We also have to compute a negative NPV using a higher discount rate. This is the trial and error method of working out the IRR. The IRR will be somewhere between the two rates and can be computed, as follows:

Using a 20% present value table discount rate (we just try different rates until we end up with a negative NPV: hence the name 'trial and error').

Year	Relevant cash flows £000	PV table @ 20%	Present value £000
1	20	0.833	16,660
2	24	0.694	16,656
3	32	0.579	18,528
4	30	0.482	14,460
5	18	0.335	<u>6,030</u>
			72,334
		Less initial investment	<u>80,000</u>
		(Negative) NPV	<u>(£7,666)</u>

10% ◄── (a gap of 10%) ─────────► 20%

£13,704   (a gap of £13,704 + £7,666 = £21,370)   (£7,666)

The above line represents a gap of 10% between the two discount rates, and a gap of £21,370 between the two net present values. The internal rate of return is, therefore:

$$10\% + \frac{£13,704}{£21,370} \times 10\% \text{ gap} = 16.41\%$$

This can be very useful where there are lots of projects of different time spans and which involve investments of differing amounts.

The profitability index

This is calculated by dividing the net present value of the relevant cash flows, by the initial investment. Once again, using our earlier net present value method example, this would work out, as follows:

$$\frac{\text{NPV of cash flows}}{\text{Initial investment}} \quad \frac{£93,704}{£80,000} = 1.1713$$

The above profitability measure is simply saying that every £1 invested in the project will generate around £1.17p of net present value cash flows.

The present value of an annuity tables

For capital investment appraisal purposes the **present value of an annuity** (i.e. an identical annual sum) table's use is very limited. It can only be used where the relevant cash flows are the same each year, or the same for a number of years.

For example, the present value of an annuity of £1 for 4 years at 10% is £3.170 (as per the table). This amount, if invested today at 10%, would, taking compound interest into account produce an income of £1 at the end of each of the next four years, a total of £4. Put another way, the present value of receiving £1 at the end of each of the next four years at an interest rate of 10% is £3.170. For other annual amounts, for example, £1,000 per year, just multiply it by the appropriate rate, as illustrated below:

The present value of £1,000 at the end of each of the next 4 years at 10% would be £1,000 × 3.170 = £3,170

Taking risk into account

Risk and uncertainty can be handled using probability to view best, worst and most likely outcomes. One of the more simple methods is to use different discount rates for project with different risk categories, for example:

Risk category	Discount rate
Low	8%
Medium	12%
High	18%

Sensitivity analysis can also be used to help identify and assess risk. This uses 'what if' scenarios to test their effects upon the estimated outcomes, for example, changing one of the variables such as the selling price.

A critical review

Methods such as the payback do not take the time value of money into account. Those discounted cash flow (DCF) methods which do take it into account such as the net present value method, discounted payback method and the internal rate of return method, are considered to be better and more appropriate to the task. The various profitability methods which use the accounting profits include non-cash items such as depreciation, and some tend to average the profits out over the life of the project. Relevant cash flows do tend to vary year by year. Indeed, the first year because of high start-up expenditure could be a negative figure.

As mentioned at the outset, the financial information, for example, using one or more of the methods described and illustrated in this chapter, is just one component part of the decision-making jigsaw. Various non-financial factors have to be taken into account, for example, technical factors such as ease of maintenance and operational considerations; additional risks and problems associated with imported equipment; standardization; size and weight of the equipment; viewing the equipment in an operational setting; human, social and environmental factors.

The selection of the discount rate also presents a challenge. In many cases the rate which is selected is the company's cost of capital. This is not so easy in practice, as there are a number of cost of capital figures which can be used, for example, the weighted average cost of capital which the company intends to use in the future!

When it comes to the assessment of risk, this does involve judgement, for example, the selection of the discount rates for different risk categories.

When all the relevant cash flows have been estimated, a discount rate selected, and the net present values calculated, the resulting tabulation gives a perception of accuracy. Beware, remember, that the relevant cash flows are **only estimates!** They may be pretty close to the truth or way off target!

KEY WORDS

Time value of money	Present value
Relevant (incremental) cash flows	Depreciation
Opportunities lost	Return on capital employed (ROCE)
Payback method	Discounted cash flow (DCF)
Net present value (NPV)	Internal rate of return (IRR)
Present value of an annuity	Profitability index
Sensitivity analysis	Risk
	Only estimates

Further reading

Atrill, P. and McLaney, E., Chapter 10 *Management Accounting for Non-Specialists*, Financial Times Prentice Hall, 2001.

Chadwick, L., Chapter 10 *Management Accounting*, International Thomson Learning, 1998.

Knott, G., Part II *Financial Management*, Macmillan Business Masters, 1998.

Useful website

Business resource area/links to other websites
www.macmillan-business.co.uk

Essays and assignments

1. In relation to capital investment appraisal, explain and illustrate the concept of relevant (incremental) cash flows. [25 marks]

2. Describe and illustrate how the following methods of capital investment appraisal work, and comment briefly on their drawbacks:
   - the payback method [5 marks]
   - the net present value method [10 marks]
   - the internal rate of return method [10 marks]

3. Discuss the problems and questions which need to be resolved in order to apply capital investment appraisal methods which take the time value of money into account. [25 marks]

Data response questions

Read the information on Wood and Green Ltd and then answer the questions below.

1. (a) Analyze and comment upon Wood and Green's working capital position. [8 marks]
   (b) Evaluate ways in which the management of working capital may be improved. [12 marks]
   (c) Assume that during the year 20X3, the sales target has been reached, stock holding has been reduced to an average of 16.67% of cost sales and debtors to 45 days. Construct and comment upon a cashflow forecast for the Year 20X3. [14 marks]
   (d) Devise and justify a potential stratgey for raising the finance required to acquire and use the new machine. [12 marks]
   (e) Discuss the appropriateness of DCF as a technique for evaluating the proposed investment in the new machine. [12 marks]

(Adapted from OCR Further Accounting and Finance Specimen Paper, 2000)

Wood and Green Ltd

Wood and Green Limited have been in business manufacturing protective clothing for leisure and sports market for many years. Over the past four years they have been expanding rapidly, successfully targeting new markets in the European Union and Eastern Europe. Share capital has not been increased since they incorporated in 1995. The firm is located in Newcastle and there are only two shareholders. Francis Woods owns 60% of the share and Anne Green 40%. The growth of the company has meant that good profits have been made over the years and £1,360,00 has been ploughed back into the business. Even so the firm had to rely on both short- and long-term borrowing. A bank loan of £700,000 was negotiated in 20X2 and is secured on the premises of the business. The loan is to be repaid in seven equal annual instalments at the beginning of each year from now with interest on the outstanding balance of 12%. The balance sheet as at July 20X2 is shown in Fig. 1 and extracts from the profit and loss account are shown in Fig. 2.

Further investment is needed if the potential of new markets is to be realised. The objective is to increase turnover by 25% next year with regular steady growth in subsequent years. This forecast is based on market research by an outside agency. Francis and Anne are assuming that the cost of sale (as a percentage of sales) will remain unchanged next year.

The most important requirement is a new machine. Purchase, installation and training are estimated to cost £600,000. Both directors are well aware that sucess is going to depend on the efficient management of cashflow during the coming year. To this end, Anne Green has agreed to prepare a cashflow forecast for the next twelve months and to consider ways in which working capital management can be improved.

Figure 1 Balance Sheet: Wood and Green: As at 31 July 20X2

	£'000	£'000	£'000
Fixed assets			
Land and buildings		1,560	
Plant and machinery	1060		
Less depreciation	(480)	580	
Vehicles	216		
Less depreciation	(96)	120	2260
Current assets			
Stock	580		
Debtors	400	980	
Current liabilities			

Creditors	260		
Dividend payable	100		
Tax payable	200		
Overdraft	20	(580)	400
Net assets			2660
Financed by:			
Share capital		600	
Reserves		1360	
Bank loan		700	
			2660

Figure 2 Wood and Green Ltd profit and loss account for the year ended 31 July 20X2

	£'000	£'000
Sales		2,400
Cost of sales		980
Gross profit		1,420
Expenses	592	
Depreciation	144	
Interest on loan	84	
		(820)
Net profit before tax		600
Tax		(200)
Net profit after tax		400
Dividend payable		(100)
Retained profit		300

Conclusion

The objective of this book was to provide you with a concise, user-friendly appreciation of financial management for AS and A level, and other courses in business and management studies. Having now completed working through the book you should:

- have a reasonable knowledge of the different sources of finance available to a business, and the considerations which help to determine which source or combination of sources is most appropriate, taking into account the specific circumstances of each individual case
- have developed a good working knowledge of the three key financial accounting statements i.e. the profit and loss account, the balance sheet, and the cash flow statement
- be able to illustrate the effect of errors and/or alternative accounting treatments and/or changes in accounting policies on the profit and loss account, and balance sheet
- be able to demonstrate the need for the depreciation of fixed assets and the way in which it is accounted for
- be able to carry out a financial performance analysis using accounting ratios
- appreciate the need for cost and management accounting, for example, in planning and control, costing goods and services, pricing and decision making
- understand the use of total absorption costing, marginal costing and break-even analysis
- know and be able to describe the benefits to a company or organization of effective budgeting and budgetary control
- be able to prepare cash budgets (cash flow forecasts), budgeted profit and loss accounts, and budgeted balance sheets
- understand the concept of relevant cash flows, and be able to use capital investment appraisal techniques, such as: the pay back, the net present value method, and the internal rate of return method.

To conclude, please always try to remember that accounting is not an exact science, and that the final accounts, and financial performance analysis, can be affected by the application of accounting policies, the 'cut-off procedure', creative accounting and 'window dressing', off-balance-sheet financing, the re-valuation of assets, and so on. Also remember that in management accounting, much of the information has to be pre-determined i.e. the figures used are only estimates. The one certainty about the future is that it will be uncertain!

Net present value tables

PRESENT VALUE OF £1

Year	5%	6%	7%	8%	9%	10%	11%	12%	13%	14%	15%	16%	17%	18%	19%	20%	21%	22%	23%	24%	25%	26%	27%	28%	29%	30%	35%	40%
0	1.000	1.000	1.000	1.000	1.000	1.000	1.000	1.000	1.000	1.000	1.000	1.000	1.000	1.000	1.000	1.000	1.000	1.000	1.000	1.000	1.000	1.000	1.000	1.000	1.000	1.000	1.000	1.000
1	.952	.943	.935	.926	.917	.909	.901	.893	.885	.877	.870	.862	.855	.847	.840	.833	.826	.820	.813	.807	.800	.794	.787	.781	.775	.769	.741	.714
2	.907	.890	.873	.857	.842	.826	.812	.797	.783	.769	.756	.743	.731	.718	.706	.694	.683	.672	.661	.650	.640	.630	.620	.610	.601	.592	.549	.510
3	.864	.840	.816	.794	.772	.751	.731	.712	.693	.675	.658	.641	.624	.609	.593	.579	.564	.551	.537	.524	.512	.500	.488	.477	.466	.455	.406	.364
4	.823	.792	.763	.735	.708	.683	.659	.636	.613	.592	.572	.552	.534	.516	.499	.482	.467	.451	.437	.423	.410	.397	.384	.373	.361	.350	.301	.260
5	.784	.747	.713	.681	.650	.621	.593	.567	.543	.519	.497	.476	.456	.437	.419	.402	.386	.370	.355	.341	.328	.315	.303	.291	.280	.269	.223	.186
6	.746	.705	.666	.630	.596	.564	.535	.507	.480	.456	.432	.410	.390	.370	.352	.335	.319	.303	.289	.275	.262	.250	.238	.227	.217	.207	.165	.133
7	.711	.665	.623	.583	.547	.513	.482	.452	.425	.400	.376	.354	.333	.314	.296	.279	.263	.249	.235	.222	.210	.198	.188	.178	.168	.159	.122	.095
8	.677	.627	.582	.540	.502	.467	.434	.404	.376	.351	.327	.305	.285	.266	.249	.233	.218	.204	.191	.179	.168	.157	.148	.139	.130	.123	.091	.068
9	.645	.592	.544	.500	.460	.424	.391	.361	.333	.308	.284	.263	.243	.225	.209	.194	.180	.167	.155	.144	.134	.125	.116	.108	.101	.094	.067	.048
10	.614	.558	.508	.463	.422	.386	.352	.322	.295	.270	.247	.227	.208	.191	.176	.162	.149	.137	.126	.116	.107	.099	.092	.085	.078	.073	.050	.035
11	.585	.527	.475	.429	.388	.350	.317	.287	.261	.237	.215	.195	.178	.162	.148	.135	.123	.112	.103	.094	.086	.079	.072	.066	.061	.056	.037	.025
12	.557	.497	.444	.397	.356	.319	.286	.257	.231	.208	.187	.168	.152	.137	.124	.112	.102	.092	.083	.076	.069	.062	.057	.052	.047	.043	.027	.018
13	.530	.469	.415	.368	.326	.290	.258	.229	.204	.182	.163	.145	.130	.116	.104	.093	.084	.075	.068	.061	.055	.050	.045	.040	.037	.033	.020	.013
14	.505	.442	.388	.340	.299	.263	.232	.205	.181	.160	.141	.125	.111	.099	.088	.078	.069	.062	.055	.049	.044	.039	.035	.032	.028	.025	.015	.009
15	.481	.417	.362	.315	.275	.239	.209	.183	.160	.140	.123	.108	.095	.084	.074	.065	.057	.051	.045	.040	.035	.031	.028	.025	.022	.020	.011	.006
16	.458	.394	.339	.292	.252	.218	.188	.163	.141	.123	.107	.093	.081	.071	.062	.054	.047	.042	.036	.032	.028	.025	.022	.019	.017	.015	.008	.005
17	.436	.371	.317	.270	.231	.198	.170	.146	.125	.108	.093	.080	.069	.060	.052	.045	.039	.034	.030	.026	.023	.020	.017	.015	.013	.012	.006	.003
18	.416	.350	.296	.250	.212	.180	.153	.130	.111	.095	.081	.069	.059	.051	.044	.038	.032	.028	.024	.021	.018	.016	.014	.012	.010	.009	.005	.002
19	.396	.331	.277	.232	.194	.164	.138	.116	.098	.083	.070	.060	.051	.043	.037	.031	.027	.023	.020	.017	.014	.012	.011	.009	.008	.007	.003	.002
20	.377	.312	.258	.215	.178	.149	.124	.104	.087	.073	.061	.051	.043	.037	.031	.026	.022	.019	.016	.014	.012	.010	.008	.007	.006	.005	.002	.001
25	.295	.233	.184	.146	.116	.092	.074	.059	.047	.038	.030	.025	.020	.016	.013	.011	.009	.007	.006	.005	.004	.003	.003	.002	.002	.001	.001	.000
30	.231	.174	.131	.099	.075	.057	.044	.033	.026	.020	.015	.012	.009	.007	.005	.004	.003	.003	.002	.002	.001	.001	.001	.001	.000	.000	.000	.000
35	.181	.130	.094	.068	.049	.036	.026	.019	.014	.010	.008	.006	.004	.003	.002	.002	.001	.001	.001	.000	.000	.000	.000	.000	.000	.000	.000	.000
40	.142	.097	.067	.046	.032	.022	.015	.011	.008	.005	.004	.003	.002	.001	.001	.001	.000	.000	.000	.000	.000	.000	.000	.000	.000	.000	.000	.000
45	.111	.073	.048	.031	.021	.014	.009	.006	.004	.003	.002	.001	.001	.001	.000	.000	.000	.000	.000	.000	.000	.000	.000	.000	.000	.000	.000	.000
50	.087	.054	.034	.021	.013	.009	.005	.003	.002	.001	.001	.001	.000	.000	.000	.000	.000	.000	.000	.000	.000	.000	.000	.000	.000	.000	.000	.000

Note: The above present value factors are based on year-end interest calculations

CUMULATIVE PRESENT VALUE OF £1 PER ANNUM
(i.e. present value of an annuity of £1)

Year	5%	6%	7%	8%	9%	10%	11%	12%	13%	14%	15%	16%	17%	18%	19%	20%	21%	22%	23%	24%	25%	26%	27%	28%	29%	30%	35%	40%
1	.952	.943	.935	.926	.917	.909	.901	.893	.885	.877	.870	.862	.855	.847	.840	.833	.826	.820	.813	.807	.800	.794	.787	.781	.775	.769	.741	.714
2	1.859	1.833	1.808	1.783	1.759	1.736	1.713	1.690	1.668	1.647	1.626	1.605	1.585	1.566	1.546	1.528	1.510	1.492	1.474	1.457	1.440	1.424	1.407	1.392	1.376	1.361	1.289	1.224
3	2.723	2.673	2.624	2.577	2.531	2.487	2.444	2.402	2.361	2.322	2.283	2.246	2.210	2.174	2.140	2.106	2.074	2.042	2.011	1.981	1.952	1.923	1.896	1.868	1.842	1.816	1.696	1.589
4	3.546	3.465	3.387	3.312	3.240	3.170	3.102	3.037	2.974	2.914	2.855	2.798	2.743	2.690	2.639	2.589	2.540	2.494	2.448	2.404	2.362	2.320	2.280	2.241	2.203	2.166	1.997	1.849
5	4.329	4.212	4.100	3.993	3.890	3.791	3.696	3.605	3.517	3.433	3.352	3.274	3.199	3.127	3.058	2.991	2.926	2.864	2.804	2.745	2.689	2.635	2.583	2.532	2.483	2.436	2.220	2.035
6	5.076	4.917	4.767	4.623	4.486	4.355	4.231	4.111	3.998	3.889	3.784	3.685	3.589	3.498	3.410	3.326	3.245	3.167	3.092	3.021	2.951	2.885	2.821	2.759	2.700	2.643	2.385	2.168
7	5.786	5.582	5.389	5.206	5.033	4.868	4.712	4.564	4.423	4.288	4.160	4.039	3.922	3.812	3.706	3.605	3.508	3.416	3.327	3.242	3.161	3.083	3.009	2.937	2.868	2.802	2.508	2.263
8	6.463	6.210	5.971	5.747	5.535	5.335	5.146	4.968	4.799	4.639	4.487	4.344	4.207	4.078	3.954	3.837	3.726	3.619	3.518	3.421	3.329	3.241	3.156	3.076	2.999	2.925	2.598	2.331
9	7.108	6.802	6.515	6.247	5.995	5.759	5.537	5.328	5.132	4.946	4.772	4.607	4.451	4.303	4.163	4.031	3.905	3.786	3.673	3.566	3.463	3.366	3.273	3.184	3.100	3.019	2.665	2.379
10	7.722	7.360	7.024	6.710	6.418	6.145	5.889	5.650	5.426	5.216	5.019	4.833	4.659	4.494	4.339	4.192	4.054	3.923	3.799	3.682	3.571	3.465	3.366	3.269	3.178	3.092	2.715	2.414
11	8.306	7.887	7.499	7.139	6.805	6.495	6.207	5.938	5.687	5.453	5.234	5.029	4.836	4.656	4.486	4.327	4.177	4.035	3.902	3.776	3.656	3.544	3.437	3.335	3.239	3.147	2.752	2.438
12	8.863	8.384	7.943	7.536	7.161	6.814	6.492	6.194	5.918	5.660	5.421	5.197	4.988	4.793	4.610	4.439	4.278	4.127	3.985	3.851	3.725	3.606	3.493	3.387	3.286	3.190	2.779	2.456
13	9.394	8.853	8.358	7.904	7.487	7.103	6.750	6.424	6.122	5.842	5.583	5.342	5.118	4.910	4.715	4.533	4.362	4.203	4.053	3.912	3.780	3.656	3.538	3.427	3.322	3.223	2.799	2.469
14	9.899	9.295	8.745	8.244	7.786	7.367	6.982	6.628	6.302	6.002	5.724	5.468	5.229	5.008	4.802	4.611	4.432	4.265	4.108	3.962	3.824	3.695	3.573	3.459	3.351	3.249	2.814	2.478
15	10.380	9.712	9.108	8.559	8.061	7.606	7.191	6.811	6.462	6.142	5.847	5.575	5.324	5.092	4.876	4.675	4.490	4.315	4.153	4.001	3.859	3.726	3.601	3.483	3.373	3.268	2.825	2.484
16	10.838	10.106	9.447	8.851	8.313	7.824	7.379	6.974	6.604	6.265	5.954	5.669	5.405	5.162	4.938	4.730	4.536	4.357	4.190	4.033	3.887	3.751	3.623	3.503	3.390	3.283	2.834	2.489
17	11.274	10.477	9.763	9.122	8.544	8.022	7.549	7.120	6.729	6.373	6.047	5.749	5.475	5.222	4.990	4.775	4.576	4.391	4.219	4.059	3.910	3.771	3.640	3.518	3.403	3.295	2.840	2.492
18	11.690	10.828	10.059	9.372	8.756	8.201	7.702	7.250	6.840	6.467	6.128	5.818	5.534	5.273	5.033	4.812	4.608	4.419	4.243	4.080	3.928	3.786	3.654	3.529	3.413	3.304	2.844	2.494
19	12.085	11.158	10.336	9.604	8.950	8.365	7.839	7.366	6.938	6.550	6.198	5.877	5.584	5.316	5.070	4.844	4.635	4.442	4.263	4.097	3.942	3.799	3.666	3.539	3.421	3.311	2.848	2.496
20	12.462	11.470	10.594	9.818	9.129	8.514	7.963	7.469	7.025	6.623	6.259	5.929	5.628	5.353	5.101	4.870	4.657	4.460	4.279	4.110	3.954	3.808	3.673	3.546	3.427	3.316	2.850	2.497
25	14.094	12.783	11.654	10.675	9.823	9.077	8.422	7.843	7.330	6.873	6.464	6.097	5.766	5.467	5.195	4.948	4.721	4.514	4.323	4.147	3.985	3.834	3.694	3.564	3.442	3.329	2.856	2.499
30	15.372	13.765	12.409	11.258	10.274	9.427	8.694	8.055	7.496	7.003	6.566	6.177	5.829	5.517	5.235	4.979	4.746	4.534	4.339	4.160	3.995	3.842	3.701	3.569	3.447	3.332	2.857	2.500
35	16.374	14.498	12.948	11.655	10.567	9.644	8.855	8.176	7.586	7.070	6.617	6.215	5.858	5.539	5.251	4.992	4.756	4.541	4.345	4.164	3.998	3.845	3.703	3.571	3.448	3.333	2.857	2.500
40	17.159	15.046	13.332	11.925	10.757	9.779	8.951	8.244	7.634	7.105	6.642	6.234	5.871	5.548	5.258	4.997	4.760	4.544	4.347	4.166	3.999	3.846	3.703	3.571	3.448	3.333	2.857	2.500
45	17.774	15.456	13.606	12.108	10.881	9.863	9.008	8.283	7.661	7.123	6.654	6.242	5.877	5.552	5.261	4.999	4.761	4.545	4.347	4.166	4.000	3.846	3.704	3.571	3.448	3.333	2.857	2.500
50	18.256	15.762	13.801	12.234	10.962	9.915	9.042	8.305	7.675	7.133	6.661	6.246	5.880	5.554	5.262	5.000	4.762	4.545	4.348	4.167	4.000	3.846	3.704	3.571	3.448	3.333	2.857	2.500

Note: The above present value factors are based on year-end interest calculations

Index